DRAWING CLOSER GROWING STRONGER

DRAWING CLOSER

Making the Most of Your Walk with God

GROWING STRONGER

DON ANDERSON

MULTNOMAH BOOKS SISTERS, OREGON

DRAWING CLOSER, GROWING STRONGER

published by Multnomah Books
a part of the Questar publishing family

International Standard Book Number: 1-57673-075-1

Printed in the United States of America

Cover illustration by Charlie Hill
Cover design by Kevin Keller
Edited by Nancy Norris
Interior design by Ellen Cummings

For information:
Questar Publishers, Inc., PO Box 1720, Sisters, Oregon 97759

Library of Congress Cataloging–in–Publication Data
Anderson, Don, 1933-
Drawing closer, growing stronger: making the most of your walk with God/by Don Anderson. p.cm. Includes bibliographical references.
ISBN 1-57673-075-1 (alk. paper) 1. Christian life. I. Title.
BV4501.2.A465 1997 97-3102
248.4--DC21 CIP

97 98 99 00 01 02 03 04 — 10 9 8 7 6 5 4 3 2 1

To Pearl, my high country honey!
You've worked alongside me during conferences
and summer camps, giving your time, energy, and
talents as unto the Lord.

You've faithfully prayed for me, our five offspring, their
spouses, and our grandchildren. I pay tribute to you
for staying steady through every crisis and encouraging
us all to follow His steps.

Contents

ACKNOWLEDGMENTS

First of all, the publishing team: Don Jacobson, Dan Benson, Larry Libby, Blake Weber, Michele Tennesen, Carol Bartley, and other unnamed heroes at Questar. Special thanks to Thomas Womack for your encouragement. All of you are true partners in ministry!

The Ministries' board of directors: Twenty-five couples who sacrifice treasure, time, and talent so Pearl and I can be free to teach God's Word. For twenty-five years, your faith has kept us singing, "To God be the Glory, great things He hath done."

The office staff: Pat Graham, Jean Powell, and Genevieve Martin. Thank you for carrying out your responsibilities with such dignity and efficiency. You ladies are an asset to our ministry.

My accountability buddies: Terry Ledbetter, Randy Wolff, Leonard David, Bill Biesel, Dick Crews, Alex Moore, and Jim Austin. Thanks for caring enough to help me face the tough issues.

Soldiers in my foxhole: Bill Lawrence and Dick Knarr. Thanks for your perseverance, always being there, and urging me to finish the race with fervor.

Fran Sandin: Thanks for believing in the message I am trying to communicate. To a preacher who is prone to deal in glittering generalities, you are tough. Your tenacious spirit—prompting me to focus on the main point, illustrate it, and hammer it home—is reflected on every page.

Nancy Norris: Your editorial skills have refined and clarified the manuscript. Thank you for your insights and expertise.

Doug and Sara Boyd: Thanks for providing your place on Little Cayman so we could give birth to the first draft.

Rick and Betsy Aubrey: Pearl and I enjoyed your condo on South Padre for the rewrite, reflection, and rest.

Jane, Karen, and Doug Mackinnon: Thank you for generously sharing John's testimony. Witnessing your stability in the storm is an inspiration to all of us.

Introduction

Lives of great men, all remind us we can make our lives sublime,
and departing leave behind us footprints in the sands of time.

HENRY WADSWORTH LONGFELLOW

The flickering candle casts shadows upon the stone prison wall. Silhouetted in the dank cell is the figure of a man writing his last will and testament. Outside, daylight turns to dark while he is absorbed in his task. The prisoner is unaware of the hour, not even noticing the fading sunlight filtering through one small grate near the ceiling. Days and nights intertwine on Death Row.

"I also suffer these things, but I am not ashamed; for I know whom I have believed and I am convinced that He is able to guard what I have entrusted to Him until that day" (2 Tim. 1:12).

Who is this prisoner? By now you've probably guessed. It's the apostle Paul who expresses no panic or anxiety in his words, only peace. He knows the Sovereign God has a pattern and a plan for his life. The circumstances are just part of it.

In modern lingo we might say it's late in the game, one second left on the clock; and Paul is six points behind. The T-shirt he wears amazingly announces: NO FEAR!

Have you ever wondered how you will handle your final days? What will truly be important as you reach the threshold of eternity? Will you have any regrets?

Perhaps you have just received Christ and you have an

intense desire to draw closer to Him. You may be asking—What do I do now as a Christian? What are my responsibilities in my relationship with Christ? How can I grow stronger in Him? Possibly you have been a Christian for quite some time, yet find yourself wandering in a wilderness of your own making. You long to live fully for Jesus so that at the close of life you, like Paul, will have no remorse.

How can you accomplish this goal? Paul burned the midnight oil writing passionately to his younger pastor friend, Timothy, urging him to be strengthened by the grace of Christ Jesus and to be a good steward of the gospel. The seasoned saint knew the spiritual map well and he carefully pointed out the way to Timothy and to us.

In his writing, Paul includes three illustrations—the soldier, the athlete, and the farmer—to help us understand what is involved in completing the journey of the Christian life and in delighting the heart of God in the process.

Like a soldier we prepare for war. Our battle weapons and wardrobe are vital. Like an athlete we diligently train to triumph. Like a farmer we steadfastly cultivate the soil, sow the seed, and wait for the harvest.

Paul stands as a role model for Timothy and for us. He paved the way. He paid the price. Let's examine the footprints of the soldier, the athlete, and the farmer to see how to fight and win the war, go for the gold, bear fruit, and reap an abundant harvest.

If this is your desire, too, turn the page and, like Paul, let's begin to draw closer and grow stronger.

PART ONE

The Soldier

Chapter One

Beginning Basic Training

But as many as received Him, to them He gave the right to become children of God, even to those who believe in His name.

John 1:12

Rick arrives at boot camp with a combination of tension and torment. He wonders, What are they going to make me do? Will I be able to pull it off?

Then he lines up with other recruits to be "kitted out" with piles of strange uniforms and gear. He ponders, How do I wear this? When do I salute?

After a few weeks of intensive physical conditioning, discipline, and instruction, Rick becomes acquainted with the basics of military life. He soon learns a new vocabulary along with how to handle equipment and what it takes to win a war.

Christians also need a crash course on commitment and what it means to follow Christ. They may be curious about how to use their new Bibles, hymnbooks, and prayer lists. Perhaps they find the new terminology puzzling. Just as a fresh recruit needs training, so the new or renewed believer needs help in learning the practicalities of marching in God's army.

But what is a Christian, anyway? It might be easier to begin with what a Christian is NOT.

MISCONCEPTIONS ABOUT CHRISTIANITY

Some people believe that everybody in America is a Christian. Others think Christianity is our national religion like baseball used to be our national pastime. Some assume one who does good deeds all the time is a Christian. A growing number tag Christians as long-faced people who can't have any fun because they are restricted from doing anything enjoyable. Another misconception is that being a Christian means being a self-made man—doing the best with what you have. Wrong!

WHO IS A CHRISTIAN?

The truth is, Christians aren't self-made, they are God-made. But how? Jesus Christ accepts the penalty for our sin and declares us righteous.

Envision a courtroom scene in which the witness has just taken the stand. Listen. He's taking the oath: "I solemnly swear to tell the truth, the whole truth, and nothing but the truth, so help me God."

The prosecuting attorney turns to the witness and asks, "Have you ever seen the defendant, Donald E. Anderson, committing an act of sin?"

The witness blurts out condemning words. "I tell you, not only have I seen him committing acts of sin, he is made of sin, and he comes from a long line of sinners." Other witnesses are called; more sin is revealed. After the jury deliberates for a while, they file back into the courtroom.

The judge requests the verdict. The jury foreman stands and declares, "We, the jury, find this defendant, Donald E. Anderson, guilty on all counts of sin as charged. We recommend the death penalty."

"The law mandates the death penalty," the judge declares as he asks the trembling defendant to rise for sentencing. The judge pauses, and a voice from the back of the courtroom pierces the silence. "Your Honor, wait. Please wait."

The judge recognizes the voice of his only son. "Your Honor, if it pleases the court, I would like to take Mr. Anderson's place and suffer his punishment. I would also like to request that You, My Father, the Judge, authorize the defendant, Donald E. Anderson, to assume all the rights and privileges of being Your son."

Such a legal transaction happens to anyone who is *justified* or literally made right in God's sight by faith. Jesus steps in to pay the penalty for our guilt before a holy God. So Christianity is simply receiving Christ, God's Son. Through faith in Him we can experience all the rights and privileges of sonship. We'll suffer none of the eternal consequences of being members of a flawed, sin-filled human race.

Admitting we are sinners is tough. Our pride gets in the way. Yet, nothing we can do or say will make us perfect or acceptable to God. Unlike the old children's poem, we are not "every day in every way getting better and better."

The Scripture says:

> There is no one righteous, not even one. (Rom. 3:10)
> All have sinned and fall short of the glory of God. (Rom. 3:23)
> The wages of sin is death, but the gift of God is eternal life in Christ Jesus our Lord. (Rom. 6:23)

Because God loves us, He sent His Son to provide a means of acceptance, forgiveness of sins, life with Him instead of away from Him. That Son, Jesus—

Voluntarily surrendered the splendors of heaven for the dusty hovels of earth;

Was conceived of the Holy Spirit and born of a virgin;

Was birthed in blood and tears, like any human being;

Adopted the limitations of humanity—embracing sorrow, weariness, hunger, and thirst;

And He lived a perfect life—something only God's divine nature could accomplish.

Then Jesus, as the Lamb of God, died a sacrificial death on the cross. For three hours one Friday He suffered the sheer, unutterable loneliness of being separated from His heavenly Father for the first—and last—time.

Isaiah the prophet foreshadowed the scene seven hundred years before that day: "Surely he took up our infirmities and carried our sorrows, yet we considered him stricken by God, smitten by him, and afflicted. But he was pierced for our transgressions, he was crushed for our iniquities; the punishment that brought us peace was upon him, and by his wounds we are healed. We all, like sheep, have gone astray, each of us has turned to his own way; and the LORD has laid on him the iniquity of us all" (Isa. 53:4–6 NIV).

Because of all this, we have the potential to be made right in God's sight. When we simply believe that Jesus died for us, we are qualified to enter God's presence.

According to J. Vernon McGee, "Justification is that act of God that declares a sinner righteous by faith on the merit of Christ's sacrifice. It is the addition of the righteousness of Christ as well as the subtraction of sin."[1]

Isn't it interesting that salvation involves mathematics? The penalty of sin is subtracted; His righteousness is added. Results? We sinners become acceptable in His sight and will spend eternity with Him.

So when we stand before a holy God, we do not claim to be good or blameless, but we stand dressed in His righteousness alone. He becomes our court-appointed attorney to win our day in court. It is who He is and what He has done that brings the favorable verdict from the throne. No one else is qualified.

Without Jesus we've had it. We'll lose our case and pay the full penalty of the law. But in Christ we can proclaim with Jude: "Now to him who is able to keep you from falling and to present you before his glory *without fault* and with unspeakable joy, to the only God, our saviour, be glory and majesty, power and authority, through Jesus Christ our Lord, before time was, now, and in all ages to come. Amen" (Jude 24–25 PHILLIPS).

After we make a decision to enter into a personal relationship with God the Father through His Son—what happens? We receive a basic benefits package which includes peace, access, hope, and assurance.

PEACE

The word peace evokes images of calm, tranquillity, silence, and freedom from stress or mental disturbance. In another sense, we think of peace as an agreement made between contending parties to cease hostilities.

God and man in his fallen state are estranged. The lines are clearly drawn between the righteous Creator and the rebellious creature. "And the path of peace have they not known" (Rom. 3:17).

But through Christ we are reconciled to God. In other words, we are no longer separated or at odds. Choosing to trust Christ has its rewards. Peace and unity reign where rebellion or indifference once ruled.

Our peace is made possible because Christ washed our sins away with His blood. The apostle Paul says we have "made peace through the blood of His cross" (Col. 1:20).

Just as the word *justification* is the legal term used to describe God's love, *atonement* explains His love in the temple. In the Old Testament Jewish tabernacle, the high priest entered the holy of holies once a year on the Day of Atonement. He symbolically repented for the sins of the nation of Israel by sprinkling an animal's blood on the mercy seat. If God accepted the blood offering, the priest exited safely, and the nation was temporarily reconciled to God. Each year the priest repeated the procedure.

The sacrifice of the unblemished animal in the Old Testament foreshadowed the day when Jesus, God's perfect Son would come and take on human flesh—emptying Himself and taking the form of a servant. His mission? To permanently meet the righteous demands of a holy God. Jesus did this! The blood sacrifice of animals is done away. John the Baptist recognized Jesus as the perfect and final sacrifice when he said of Him, "Behold the Lamb of God who takes away the sin of the world!" (John 1:29).

Even before Jesus died for us, Isaiah the prophet foresaw the peace that comes from knowing Jesus: "For to us a child is born, to us a son is given, and the government will be on his shoulders. And he will be called Wonderful Counselor, Mighty God, Everlasting Father, Prince of Peace. Of the increase of his government and peace there will be no end. He will reign on David's throne and over his kingdom, establishing and upholding it with justice and righteousness from that time on and forever. The zeal of the Lord Almighty will accomplish this" (Isa. 9:6–7 NIV).

He said further: "The fruit of righteousness will be peace; the effect of righteousness will be quietness and confidence forever" (Isa. 32:17 NIV).

Jesus, Himself, spoke of peace in the upper room. "Peace I leave with you; My peace I give to you; not as the world gives, do

I give to you. Let not your heart be troubled, nor let it be fearful" (John 14:27).

God has made it possible for us to have peace because the blood of His only Son was a once-for-all payment for sin. Allow me to paraphrase Hebrews 10:11–12. "And every priest has stood daily ministering and offering time after time the same sacrifices, which can never take away sins; but *He,* when He offered one sacrifice for sins for all time, sat down at the right hand of God." What Jesus did was enough. We need only accept the gift in simple childlike faith. A popular hymn expresses it this way:

> Jesus paid it all,
> All to Him I owe;
> Sin had left a crimson stain,
> He washed it white as snow.[2]

Another Scripture from Isaiah reassures us: "'Come now, let us reason together,' says the LORD. 'Though your sins are like scarlet, they shall be as white as snow; though they are red as crimson, they shall be like wool'" (Isa. 1:18 NIV).

ACCESS

Not only do we have peace as a result of our relationship with Jesus Christ, we are invited into the very presence of God by faith.

Access is the privilege of coming into the presence of another. It is coming home, bounding into the house, greeting the family, sitting at the supper table, and discussing the day's events with our beloved. So it is with God. Through faith, we have the privilege of coming into His presence, talking with Him, and having Him communicate with us. We have access!

Peace precedes access. Because I have a relationship with my wife and children, I have access into our home. Otherwise I would have to knock at the door, wait, and seek permission to enter. So a relationship with the Father gives us admittance.

Why? When Jesus died on the cross, the veil separating the holy of holies in the Old Testament tabernacle was shredded in two. In those days, only the priest was allowed to enter the holy of holies. But at Jesus' death, God reached down and ripped the tremendous curtain from top to bottom.

God's action here bears witness to the fact that He is fully satisfied with the work of His Son and that anyone who believes may come into His presence by means of, a "new and living way" (Heb. 10:19–20). It is new because it was not there before. It is living because it ushers in life through a living Savior.

Thus the body of Jesus Christ was broken and the veil rent so we can have peace with God and access into His presence. Through the blood of Jesus the sin chasm is bridged, separation between God and man is spanned through Him.

This means that as Christians we may pray anytime—day or night—and know that God hears and understands. In the words of the hymn writer:

> Oh, the love that drew salvation's plan!
> Oh, the grace that brought it down to man!
> Oh, the mighty gulf that God did span
> At Calvary![3]

HOPE

The life of Jesus did not end at the cross. He arose. His resurrection gives us hope. "Blessed be the God and Father of our Lord Jesus Christ, who according to His great mercy has caused us to be born again to a living hope through the resurrection of Jesus Christ from the dead" (1 Pet. 1:3).

So the third manifestation of an eternal transaction is ongoing hope in the living God. "We exult in hope of the glory of God," exclaims Paul (Rom. 5:2).

Hope is an expectation of something desired. Do you remember as a kid making a Christmas list of your desires? (I still make 'em.) Our desires were accompanied by the expectation of finding at least some of the requested stuff under the tree Christmas morning. We anticipated satisfaction. In other words, we hoped.

A relationship with Jesus produces hope as well. Hope of heaven. Hope of His presence. Hope of His finished work. Sometimes we didn't get everything we'd hoped for at Christmas, but our hope in Christ is sure and never changing. These verses explain:

> This hope we have as an anchor of the soul, a hope both sure and steadfast and one which enters within the veil. (Heb. 6:19)
>
> For you have been my hope, O Sovereign LORD, my confidence since my youth. (Ps. 71:5 NIV)
>
> I wait for you, O LORD; you will answer, O LORD my God. (Ps. 38:15 NIV)
>
> But now, LORD, what do I look for? My hope is in you. (Ps. 39:7 NIV)

Jesus Himself testifies to this hope: "Let not your heart be troubled; believe in God, believe also in Me. In My Father's house are many dwelling places; if it were not so, I would have told you; for I go to prepare a place for you. And if I go and prepare a place for you, I will come again and receive you to Myself; that where I am, there you may be also" (John 14:1–3).

What sustained the apostle Paul through all his trials and testings? Hope. While nearing the end of his life, he writes his second epistle to Timothy. As he reflects on his ministry, he is pleased that he fought the good fight, finished the course, and kept the faith. He also looks forward with hope and joy to his time in heaven. As believers we, too, have this hope.

ASSURANCE

Peace, access, and hope are evidences of receiving Christ. Another is the assurance of salvation—of knowing that we've received the Savior. Then we can honestly sing:

> Blessed assurance, Jesus is mine!
> Oh, what a foretaste of glory divine!
> Heir of salvation, purchase of God,
> Born of His Spirit, washed in His blood.[4]

The word *assurance* means to have confidence, freedom from doubt, certainty. The Bible teaches that Christians do have assurance that they belong to Christ forever. They can never be torn from His hand. Yet, too many of us question and doubt and fail to act as if this were true.

We can have assurance about our relationship with Jesus. Really. We can *know* we are children of God.

These verses help us understand assurance:

> And we desire that each one of you show the same diligence so as to realize the full assurance of hope until the end. (Heb. 6:11)
> By this we know that we abide in Him and He in us, because He has given us of His Spirit. (1 John 4:13)
> But whoever keeps His word, in him the love of God has truly been perfected. By this we know that we are in Him. (1 John 2:5)

> My sheep hear My voice, and I know them, and they follow Me; and I give eternal life to them, and they shall never perish; and no one shall snatch them out of My hand. (John 10:27–28)

It is sometimes hard to believe that a relationship with Christ is both free and permanent. As a pastor and Bible teacher, people often ask me questions about assurance. Here are a few answers I provide.

CAN WE REALLY KNOW BEFORE WE DIE THAT OUR DESTINATION IS HEAVEN?

Yes, we can. The following biblical examples of assurance are given. These men knew:

JOB: "I know that my Redeemer lives, and that in the end he will stand upon the earth. And after my skin has been destroyed, yet in my flesh I will see God; I myself will see him with my own eyes—I and not another. How my heart yearns within me!" (Job 19:25–27 NIV).

DAVID: "Even though I walk through the valley of the shadow of death, I will fear no evil, for you are with me; your rod and your staff, they comfort me" (Ps. 23:4 NIV).

PAUL: "For I am convinced that neither death, nor life, nor angels, nor principalities, nor things present, nor things to come, nor powers, nor height, nor depth, nor any other created thing, shall be able to separate us from the love of God, which is in Christ Jesus our Lord" (Rom. 8:38–39).

If they knew and we can know, why don't more people seem to know? One reason may be that they have never received Jesus Christ as Savior by a simple act of faith.

Some people substitute external things for a relationship with God. Man looks on the outward appearance; God looks on the heart. Church membership, baptism, a perfect Sunday school attendance pin, a Christian family—all these good things may stand in the way of our humbly coming before God and acknowledging our sin and our need of the Savior. If we never really come clean, we have no assurance.

As long as our relationship with God is based on human performance, we will never be assured of our eternal destiny. We are saved by faith, not good deeds. According to the apostle Paul: "For by grace you have been saved through faith; and that not of yourselves, it is the gift of God; not as a result of works, that no one should boast" (Eph. 2:8–9).

Can we know our destination will be heaven? Because of Christ, the answer is a resounding "Yes!"

WHY DON'T I FEEL SAVED?

Another cause of doubt is that people may not *feel* they are in an eternally secure relationship. If we don't feel saved, perhaps we are placing too much emphasis on feeling! God's order is fact, faith, and then feeling, but sometimes we reverse it.

In Acts 8:26–40 Philip meets an Ethiopian eunuch. Talk about a sovereign appointment! He just *happens* to be reading Isaiah 53 when Philip arrives on the scene. Philip begins by telling him facts about Jesus. Then comes faith as the eunuch believes in the Lord Jesus Christ. Later the Ethiopian eunuch goes on his way rejoicing. First comes fact, then faith, then feeling. Don't overemphasize feelings—they can be misleading.

The simple poem "Fact, Faith, Feeling" reminds us.

"One day Mr. Fact, Mr. Faith, and Mr. Feeling were walking along a wall. Mr. Fact was first, Mr. Faith second, and Mr. Feeling was tagging along behind. Whenever Mr. Feeling took his eyes off

Mr. Fact and Mr. Faith, he fell off the wall. But as long as he kept his eyes on Mr. Fact and Mr. Faith, he stayed on the wall."[5]

The fact is God said Jesus died for us. We believe it. That settles it.

SO HOW CAN WE KNOW WE ARE ETERNALLY SECURE?

We know we belong to God because:

> We remember trusting Jesus. If we don't recall an exact date or time, we can ask ourselves a question like this: "Whom am I trusting right now for salvation?"
>
> We are secure by the authority of the word of God. "And the witness is this, that God has given us eternal life, and this life is in His Son. He who has the Son has the life; he who does not have the Son of God does not have the life" (1 John 5:11–12).
>
> We have love for our brothers and sisters in the body of Christ. "A new commandment I give to you, that you love one another even as I have loved you, that you also love one another. By this all men will know that you are My disciples if you have love one for another" (John 13:34–35).
>
> The third person of the Trinity, the Holy Spirit, has come to dwell within. "The Spirit Himself bears witness with our spirit that we are children of God. And if children, heirs also, heirs of God and fellow heirs with Christ, if indeed we suffer with Him in order that we may also be glorified with Him" (Rom. 8:16–17).

The Spirit of God becomes the inner endorsement that we are children of God. We sense His conviction and His presence. He grieves over sin that occurs in our lives after we become believers, and He opens our eyes so we may behold wondrous things from the word of God.

WHAT HAPPENS ONCE WE ARE SURE?

We'll have joy and victory! "But thanks be to God, who gives us the victory through our Lord Jesus Christ" (1 Cor. 15:57). We'll see the evidence as the Spirit reveals truths from God's Word. We'll grow spiritually. "Long to grow up into the fullness of your salvation; cry for this as a baby cries for his milk" (1 Pet. 2:3 TLB).

OUR RESPONSE

After hearing the plan of salvation, each person makes a choice. Remember the courtroom scene? We have the option of refusing the Savior's pardon, continuing our own course, and taking our chances with the judge.

Jesus concludes His sermon on the mount with the story of two men. One opts to build his house upon the sand and the other chooses to build his house upon the rock. When the rains and the floods came, the house upon the sand falls and great is the fall of it. But when the storms and the floods come, the house upon the rock stands firm.

Jesus is the rock. Choosing Him is a timely decision. From then on our lives are built upon a firm foundation. As Pastor Tony Evans so aptly warns, "When it's raining, it's too late to pour concrete."

In the military service, basic training is rigorous, grueling, and scheduled for a limited time. In the Christian life, understanding the basics is foundational, but growth is a process. Instant maturity is unavailable for Christians. However, getting to know the Commander-in-Chief will keep us focused and strong.

CHAPTER TWO

Getting to Know the Commander-in-Chief

I count all things to be loss in view of the surpassing value of knowing Christ Jesus my Lord.

PHILIPPIANS 3:8

Despite his busy schedule during the Civil War, Abraham Lincoln often visited the hospitals to cheer the wounded. On one occasion he saw a young fellow who was near death.

"Is there anything I can do for you?" asked the compassionate president.

"Please write a letter to my mother," came the reply.

Unrecognized by the soldier, the chief executive sat down and wrote as the youth told him what to say. The letter read:

> My Dearest Mother,
>
> I was badly hurt while doing my duty, and I won't recover.
>
> Don't sorrow too much for me. May God bless you and Father. Kiss Mary and John for me.

The young man was too weak to go on, so Lincoln signed the letter for him and then added this postscript: Written for your son by Abraham Lincoln.

Asking to see the note, the soldier was astonished to discover who had shown him such kindness. "Are you really our president?" he asked.

"Yes," was the quiet answer. "Now, is there anything else I can do?"

The lad feebly replied, "Will you hold my hand? I think it would help see me through to the end."

The tall, gaunt man granted his request, offering warm words of encouragement until death stole in with the dawn.[1]

Before this event, the young soldier had known *about* the Commander-in-Chief of the armed forces, but he had not heard his voice, experienced his presence, nor felt his touch. Then he met him *personally*.

The apostle Paul writes that he considers all things loss except the "surpassing worth of the knowledge of Christ Jesus my Lord." His first priority is to know Christ by experience.

The word *knowledge* means more than surface information. It suggests experiential, personal communion, the most trusted relationship on earth, even closer than a husband and wife. Notice Paul does not say he wants to know about Jesus; rather he wants to *know* Jesus! Is it possible to recognize and understand him? In my experience, knowing Jesus is more than possible—it is an exciting reality.

Through reading His Word and communing with Him in conversational prayer, I am continually drawing closer and growing more intimate with the Savior. You can know Him too. Here's how.

STUDY THE MANUAL

A good soldier studies the military manual. He commits sections of instruction to memory. He examines the guidebook to make sure he knows what supplies will be needed for the next campaign. Then he checks his backpack. When on the field, a good soldier knows exactly what is expected of him. In a similar way, Christians have what we might call an Owner's Manual—which is God's Word. Since God designed us as human beings with all our complexities, He knows how we will operate best in day-to-day life.A popular illustration used by a well-known Christian organization, the Navigators, helps clarify what is involved in knowing God's word. Picture a hand. This hand reveals the essential elements of getting a grip on the word of God. The thumb and four fingers are labeled with the following instructions concerning Scripture:

> Hear God's Word.
> Read God's Word.
> Study God's Word.
> Memorize God's Word.
> Meditate upon God's Word.

Just as we cannot hold our Bibles with two fingers, we need all five disciplines to increase our grasp of Scripture. Why is it so important? Paul writes the answer to Timothy—"All Scripture is inspired by God and profitable for teaching, for reproof, for correction, for training in righteousness" (2 Tim. 3:16).

David was a man of the Word: "How can a young man keep his way pure? By living according to your word. I seek you with all my heart; do not let me stray from your commands. I have hidden your word in my heart that I might not sin against you" (Ps. 119:9–11 NIV). The law of the Lord was his central focus: "Blessed is the man who does not walk in the counsel of the wicked or stand in the way of sinners or sit in the seat of mockers. But his delight is in the law of the Lord, and on his law he meditates day and night. He is like a tree planted by streams of water, which yields its fruit in season and whose leaf does not wither. Whatever he does prospers" (Ps. 1:1–3 NIV).

Hear God's Word

Scripture tells us that hearing God's Word increases our faith. "So faith comes from hearing, and hearing by the word of Christ" (Rom. 10:17).

This means availing oneself of the many opportunities for exposure to God's Word from the pulpit, in Bible classes, on radio and TV, on cassette tapes, and in books. Many folks plug into taped Bible studies while commuting in traffic, doing housework, even while exercising. I'm convinced God is delighted with Sony Walkmans.

God's word is intriguing! One prison warden wrote to our ministry and told us a young inmate had been listening to a series of our tapes on the life of Joseph. The day of his release he told the warden, "Man, I hate to leave. I won't get to finish those tapes and find out what happened to Joseph!"

In addition to Bible studies on tape, the narrated version of the entire Bible, verse by verse, is now available. Some people who are ill and unable to read find listening to God's Word very comforting.

Read God's Word

Reading scripture is as important as hearing it. Literally hundreds of formats of the Bible are available for any age group or gender. We can choose from: paraphrases, verse-by-verse translations, thought-by-thought translations, special Bibles for moms, dads, teens, couples, even folks with addictive behaviors. Most Christian bookstores carry a wide selection.

When we read Scripture we are nourishing our spirits. While we may not *feel* any different at the time, we are gradually gaining a better understanding of the character of God and of how He wants us to respond to everyday situations in life. I try to read through different versions of the Bible in my devotional times. It makes my time in the Word rich and exciting. Unexpected phrases will jump out of the text and begin ministering to my heart.

Over the years of studying and teaching God's Word, numerous times I have witnessed lives being changed before my very eyes through exposure to the Word—including the ladies who type my lecture notes, students in my classes, and discipleship encounters.

"As the rain and the snow come down from heaven, and do not return to it without watering the earth and making it bud and flourish, so that it yields seed for the sower and bread for the eater, so is my word that goes out from my mouth: It will not return to me empty, but will accomplish what I desire and achieve the purpose for which I sent it" (Isa. 55:10–11 NIV).

"And for this reason we also constantly thank God that when you received from us the word of God's message, you accepted it not as the word of men, but for what it really is, the word of God, which also performs its work in you who believe" (1 Thess. 2:13). After Paul left Thessalonica, he had a real treat in store when he got to Berea: "Now these were more noble-minded than those in Thessalonica, for they received the word with great eagerness, examining the Scriptures daily, to see whether these things were so" (Acts 17:11). The centrality of the Scriptures is key to any spiritual growth. Listen to Jeremiah: "When your words came, I ate them; they were my joy and my heart's delight, for I bear your name, O LORD God Almighty" (Jer. 15:16 NIV).

Study God's Word

"Be diligent to present yourself approved to God as a workman who does not need to be ashamed, handling accurately the word of truth" (2 Tim. 2:15).

Paul writes to Timothy telling him to make every effort to be a student of God's Word. This involves sweat and study. It involves asking questions such as:

1. What do I see? (Observation)
2. What does it mean? (Interpretation)
3. What does it mean to me? (Application)

Or we can simply ask who? What? When? Where? How? Keeping a notebook and pen handy is important for jotting insights, words, or key phrases. A Bible dictionary, concordance, and other reference tools will help when digging deeper into a verse or passage.

I will always remember how rich and timely my first word study in the Greek text was to me personally. My assignment was to dig into the full meaning of the word *depart* in Philippians 1:23. I never realized one word could be so interesting.

After looking up the word, I discovered Paul is saying to the saints in this verse: "I am being held in custody between the two (life and death), having the desire to depart and to be with Christ for that is very much better." The phrase *to depart* has some great pictures in its meaning:

A ship untying and loosing its moorings to set sail;

A camper pulling up the tent stakes and going to his permanent dwelling.

The latter reminded me of Paul's words about death for the Christian. "For we know that if the earthly tent which is our house is torn down, we have a building from God, a house not made with hands, eternal in the heavens" (2 Cor. 5:1).

As I worked on this assignment, I was mourning the loss of one of my classmates who had been killed in a holiday car accident. He had just *departed* into eternity! What joy and peace flooded my heart as I became aware of how temporary everything is down here. This study, plus a godly professor who comforted us with these words: "Saints are immortal until their work on earth is done!" got me through my first real experience with physical death.

Prolonged exposure to Scripture changes our lives. What riches await us! God has provided all we need for right living through His Word. Our part is to mine the nuggets of truth that lie beneath the surface.

Many fine programs already exist for helping us examine Scripture. Churches often sponsor Bible studies. Some nondenominational organizations offering study helps are: Bible Study Fellowship, Campus Crusade for Christ, Intervarsity, Navigators, Precept Ministries, and others. Our own Bible study materials include over fifty different book, character, and topical studies on cassette tapes and some on video. We are presently in the process of training teachers in the Inductive Bible Study Method and supplying materials to teach the Word.

Memorize God's Word

In addition to reading and studying Scripture, we learn to memorize it. Why? "I have hidden your word in my heart that I might not sin against you," writes the psalmist (Ps. 119:11 NIV). Hiding God's Word in our hearts hastens Christian maturity. It is a purifying process.

Les, an older gentleman in one of the churches I pastored, memorized over one hundred verses his first year as a Christian. He reviewed them daily while working out on his rowing machine. He's still at it too. Jesus teaches us the importance of having the Word readily available during satanic attack. Jesus handles each of the three temptations with Scripture quoted from the book of Deuteronomy.

One easy way to get started is to write out a verse on an index card and carry it with you. Put it in an obvious place while working or getting dressed in the mornings. Learn phrase by phrase until you can repeat the verse from memory. Review it often. Quote the reference before and after each time, so you will always remember where to find it. The more you memorize, the easier the process becomes.

The Navigators also have a Topical Memory System which is an excellent beginning plan. You may even want to involve other members of your family as you ask them to test your memory on a few verses. This is a great discipline to use in your accountability and mentoring relationships.

Meditate on God's Word

Memorizing the Word provides fodder for meditation. Meditating means reflecting on concepts, filling your mind with thoughts of Scripture, and thinking about what God is saying to you. Meditation is certainly not limited to memorized passages. You can also meditate as you simply read through a passage. "But his delight is in the law of the Lord, and on his law he meditates day and night" (Ps. 1:2 NIV).

My granddaughter, Chelsea, said to me one time, "Grandpa, my tummy is growling for food."

The prophet Jeremiah felt the same way about God's word: "When your words came, I ate them; they were my joy and my heart's delight, for I bear your name, O LORD God Almighty" (Jer. 15:16 NIV). Just as our bodies need physical nourishment, our souls need spiritual food.

Seeking the Word precedes doing the Word. We must know it before we can put it into practice. Just as infants need frequent feedings, so should we be consuming Scripture on a regular, life-altering basis.

Ezra is one of my favorite Old Testament characters. One verse summarizes the secret of his spiritual maturity: "For Ezra had prepared his heart to seek the law of the LORD, and to do it, and to teach in Israel statutes and judgments" (Ezra 7:10 KJV).

Ezra prepared his heart by setting his priorities in order and devoting time to God's Word. He wanted to know God's truth and he wanted that truth to direct his path.

He didn't stop with just wanting to know God's law, he wanted to do it. Then he wanted to proclaim God's truth to others. In maturity he was able to teach others. His knowledge of God came from spending time in God's Word. In my relationship with God, He is speaking to me through His Word and my response to Him is in prayer.

Nothing is more thrilling than to wake up in the early morning hours and talk with the Father using words straight from His book. I love to lie there sensing His Presence, thinking of Him as smiling and saying, "Good morning, Don."

Then I respond with verses I have memorized: "In the morning, O LORD, you hear my voice; in the morning I lay my requests before you and wait in expectation" (Ps. 5:3 NIV).

"I rise before dawn and cry for help; I have put my hope in your word" (Ps. 119:147 NIV).

"Test me, O LORD, and try me, examine my heart and my mind; for your love is ever before me, and I walk continually in your truth" (Ps. 26:2–3 NIV).

"This is the day the LORD has made; let us rejoice and be glad in it" (Ps. 118:24 NIV).

PRAY

We may think of prayer as saying grace before meals, reciting a memorized version of The Lord's Prayer, or kneeling beside the bed to pray at bedtime. Far too many folks see prayer as a 911 panic situation, or worse yet, an 800 service to place their orders. Prayer that is filled with panic and petition without praise is more of a ritual than the outgrowth of a relationship.

Real prayer is simply a heart turned toward heaven. The Lord Jesus lives there and provides access to the Heavenly Father anytime. The more we pray, the more comfortable we become talking things over with Him. Purpose, passion, and power flow out of these precious times of communion.

Prayer involves worship, adoration, and praise. Each morning from 8:00–8:30 A.M. our staff prays together. I warned them the other day our time together on the following morning was going to be limited to praise only. We slipped into petition out of praise a couple of times, but my oh my! what joy flooded our hearts as we praised Him for His person, presence, power, program, purpose, provision, protection, and peace. (We finally had to quit because we ran out of P words.)

As we invite Him to scrutinize our hearts, we identify our sins and confess them specifically. "If we confess our sins, He is faithful and righteous to forgive us our sins and to cleanse us from all unrighteousness. If we say that we have not sinned, we make Him a liar, and His word is not in us" (1 John 1:9–10).

We also enter into prayer with an attitude of thanksgiving. "Be anxious for nothing, but in everything by prayer and supplication with thanksgiving let your requests be made known to God. And the peace of God, which surpasses all comprehension, shall guard your hearts and your minds in Christ Jesus." (Phil. 4:6–7). We may not always feel thankful, but we can approach God with thanksgiving because of His character and His grace. Paul reminds us, "In everything give thanks; for this is God's will for you in Christ Jesus" (1 Thess. 5:18).

God wants to hear our requests. Sometimes it helps to keep a list of items or people to pray about. Then when the answer comes, we can make note of it. Answered prayer is a great encouragement to our faith.

My Pearl is our prayer warrior. Hundreds of times over the years we have seen her prayers answered by miraculous provision. I believe she has literally prayed our sons and daughters-in-law into the family as our children have been led to wonderful mates.

She explains, "I began praying for the mates our children would marry when the children were very young. I prayed that:

God would bless their parents to do a good job raising them.
They would come to know Christ as Savior at an early age.
God would protect them as they were growing up.
He would order the time of their meeting, relationship, and marriage into our family.

"When I remind our children that their good choices were a result of my prayers and God's answers, they just roll their eyes. They like to think it was their good looks, charm, and great personality that brought the wonderful person into their life! When they begin praying for their own children, though, I think they'll understand.

"Another answer to prayer came when our daughter, Becky, was on dialysis due to complications caused by diabetes. She needed a kidney transplant. We prayed every day for a donor that would match. Through circumstances only God could work out, they found the perfect match in only three weeks. Some people she met at the dialysis clinic had been waiting two years or more."

A nineteen-year-old motorcycle rider in Florida had the foresight to sign a donor card and upon his death, Becky became the recipient of one of his kidneys. It has been nine years now and Becky is a miracle. Deeply in love with her wonderful husband, Ray, they are enjoying life to the fullest.

Not only has Pearl prayed diligently for our family, but the fruit of our ministry has been the direct result of her persevering prayer. When we get into an argument, it's no fun, because I always feel it's two against one, and that is lonely!

We can also look to biblical examples of people who prayed. Why was the prophet Daniel such a mighty man of God? He never quit praying. Daniel's rise to power in the Persian government came when King Darius selected Daniel to fill a choice cabinet position in his new administration. When Darius considered elevating Daniel further, Daniel's rivals heard about it and hatched a plot to get Daniel out of the way.

So they drew up hush-hush legislation prohibiting prayer to God and rushed it by Darius. Daniel kept praying and someone saw him "breaking the law." He was arrested, tossed like a lamb chop into a pit of starving lions, and you've probably heard the rest. God protected him. He curled up with those critters like they were pussy cats.

While our situation may not be like Daniel's, we may have to wrestle with hectic schedules, irritating people, and various temptations during the course of a day. How can we know God's presence through it all? Like Daniel, we can keep on praying. God will see us through. With Brother Lawrence we can practice the presence of God no matter where we are or what we are doing.

Many godly and holy men have chronicled their prayer life as an example to us today. Martin Luther was said to have spent his best three hours each day in prayer.

If we really want to be effective soldiers, we'll set aside some daily prayer and Bible study time. Of course, that requires discipline, but we'll get into that later. I believe the enemies' footsteps are getting closer. Let's grab the binoculars and view what's ahead.

CHAPTER THREE

Recognizing the Enemy's Strategies

Be of sober spirit, be on the alert. Your adversary, the devil, prowls about like a roaring lion, seeking someone to devour.

1 PETER 5:8

A Sunday morning sunrise on the Hawaiian Islands had never seemed more beautiful. Honeymooners were still cuddling as enthusiastic tourists consulted their maps and guides. Birds chirped as beachcombers, snorkelers, and surfers headed for the beach. Fragrant, fresh pineapples and mangoes decorated restaurant breakfast plates. Poinsettias bloomed in all their glory as islanders prepared for the Christmas holidays.

Then it happened. Scores of Japanese planes dotted the blue skies and began pelting the peaceful paradise with bombs, hitting Ford Island first at 7:55 A.M. A second raid at 8:55 A.M. added to the massive destruction. Terror-stricken people scattered to seek shelter as black smoke billowed upward. Our American fleet stationed at Pearl Harbor was all but destroyed. The casualty count quickly mounted to 2,409 with 1,178 wounded.

I was only eight years old at the time, but I can still remember the alarmed expressions on my parents' faces as we heard the radio news. Although we lived on the mainland, far from the destruction, we could feel the winds of war.

Early in the afternoon of Monday, December 8, 1941, President Roosevelt addressed a joint session of Congress and we listened with horror to the broadcast. He told how Japan had attacked Malay, Hong Kong, Guam, the Philippine Islands, Wake Island, and Midway Island as well as the Hawaiian Islands. Many Americans had been killed.

The President closed by saying, "Hostilities exist. There is no blinking at the fact that our people, our territory, and our interests are in grave danger. With confidence in our armed forces—with the unbounded determination of our people—we will gain the inevitable triumph—so help us God."[1]

To use President Roosevelt's words in a spiritual context—we as believers are also in danger. Our enemy is unseen. Just as the multiple Japanese attacks in World War II made it necessary to fight on several fronts, the believer finds he, too, must fight on three fronts: the world, the flesh, and the devil.

Just as Roosevelt reassured the American people over fifty years ago, we believers can also be confident in our armed forces. We, too, will gain the inevitable triumph—so help us God. With confidence in our victorious Savior we will win the war against Satan and the wickedness of this world. Christ's kingdom will prevail.

It's good to realize at the outset that conflict accompanies spiritual growth. Let's take a closer look at each front and then review our battle plan.

THE WORLD

Some say that if you become a Christian, all your problems will be over. You'll be happy, successful, and rich. However, the Bible teaches an entirely different concept. Jesus concludes His remarks to His men just hours before Calvary by saying: "These things I have spoken to you, that in Me you may have peace. In the world you have tribulation, but take courage; I have overcome the world" (John 16:33).

If we follow Christ in this life, we can expect to experience some degree of mistreatment for His sake, it goes with the territory. We may experience injustice. In His first public address, known as the Sermon on the Mount, Jesus says: "Blessed are you when men revile you, and persecute you, and say all kinds of evil against you falsely, on account of Me. Rejoice, and be glad, for your reward in heaven is great, for so they persecuted the prophets who were before you" (Matt. 5:11–12).

Anytime we suffer what seems to be an injustice because we're Christians, we'll understand more of what Jesus experienced while on earth. It is a real comfort to know that HE fully understands what we are going through.

Our Lord was rejected. "He came to His own, and those who were His own did not receive Him" (John 1:11). Some who believe in Jesus Christ may experience similar rejection from their family or friends. After the Damascus Road experience, Paul was so ostracized by everybody that Barnabas had to step forward and recommend him: "And when he had come to Jerusalem, he was trying to associate with the disciples; and they were all afraid of him, not believing that he was a disciple. But Barnabas took hold of him and brought him to the apostles and described to them how he had seen the Lord on the road, and that He had talked to him, and how at Damascus he had spoken out boldly in the name of Jesus" (Acts 9:26–27).

So much of the trouble Paul faced came from fellow Jews. He describes the cost of his commitment in the following words: "We are handicapped on all sides, but we are never frustrated; we are puzzled, but never in despair. We are persecuted, but we never have to stand it alone; we may be knocked down but we are never knocked out!" (2 Cor. 4:8–9 PHILLIPS).

Chuck Colson in his book, *A Dangerous Grace,* gives a modern-day example of the power of God's word in the midst of adversity. A young Polish pastor, Jerzy Popieluszko, delivered dynamic messages, stirring the Polish people to overthrow their Communist oppressors. "His theme was always the same: The Christian is called to overcome evil with good."[2]

In 1980 when martial law was declared in Poland, Jerzy hated the occupation of tanks and troops in the streets just as much as fellow countrymen, but he fought it using God's tactics—overcoming evil with good. On Christmas Eve, Jerzy crunched through the snow handing out cookies to the soldiers in the streets.

Then in 1984, Jerzy was unexpectedly kidnapped by secret police. Astounded, Christians gathered in Polish churches to pray. While steelworkers demanded his release and threatened to go on strike, fifty thousand people gathered to hear a tape of his last sermon.

Jerzy's mutilated and tortured body was found in the river. Yet, the gentle pastor had taught his people well because after the funeral, hundreds of thousands of Polish people marched through the streets of Warsaw—right in front of the Secret Police headquarters—carrying banners reading, "We forgive."

The impact still resounds. As they assaulted evil with good, the Communist regime crumbled. The darkness of evil was illuminated by Christians lighting the torch of God's truth and standing together.[3]

Some biblical examples of men who endured persecution include John the Baptist, Paul, and other believers who were not only rejected, but tormented for their steadfast faith. While we may not be ostracized or experience the same kind of treatment in our country, America can no longer be considered a Christian nation.

As we've moved further and further away from respect and awe of God and His Word and exalted man's opinions and views above God's, one who takes a stand for Christ may feel the sting of society's disapproval such as:

> The public school teacher who is reprimanded for mentioning Jesus;
> The college student whose faith is ridiculed by an agnostic professor;
> The mom whose family thinks she's crazy because she is excited about her new relationship with the Lord;
> The man who mentions Jesus at work and is called a hypocrite, bigot, fundamentalist, narrow-minded troublemaker;
> The dad who prays with his family in a restaurant while the folks at the next table snicker;
> The woman who hears a television or radio talk show host implying her Christian beliefs are naive, stupid, and ridiculous.

As a nation we have moved far away from our Christian foundation. In his book *When Nations Die,* Dr. Jim Black observes that across our nation intellectual elitists are systematically bankrupting the legacy of our founding fathers, offering radical, current concepts to replace the traditions of society. This new thinking includes a global ecological sensitivity, a vision of a new world order, and a liberal, extremist political system. What we are seeing, according to Black, is a systematic, concerted effort to change the world "by elitists in government, the judicial system, higher education, and the media."[4]

Since our Christian way of thinking is different, we can expect to face cultural battles on many fronts. We face private skirmishes as well. A good soldier accepts responsibility for his decisions and choices instead of making excuses.

If we realize that as Christians we will face adversity, we can be prepared. In the next chapter, we'll discuss more about our weapons and uniform for battle. In the meantime, we can be assured that our Commander-in-Chief has everything under control.

THE FLESH

A new, divine nature is imparted to one who is born again, but the old nature remains. Within every Christian is a chronic struggle between the old nature (flesh) and the new nature (energized by the Holy Spirit). A Christian wrestles with this conflict throughout life.

Paul shares his testimony about the flesh:

"For I know that nothing good dwells in me, that is, in my flesh; for the wishing is present in me, but the doing of the good is not. For the good that I wish, I do not do; but I practice the very evil that I do not wish. But if I am doing the very thing I do not wish, I am no longer the one doing it, but sin which dwells in me" (Rom. 7:18–20).

The war between the flesh and the spirit is best described this way:

FLESH	SPIRIT
Responds in disobedience	Responds in obedience
Wants my will instead of God's	Seeks God's will
Acts selfishly	Acts unselfishly
Rebellion against God	Submission to God

We quickly acknowledge the impossible task of living the

Christian life in our own human strength. It's impossible! No wonder Paul writes to new converts about this.

"Are you so foolish? After beginning with the Spirit, are you now trying to attain your goal by human effort?" (Gal. 3:3 NIV).

Each of us can examine our own hearts and identify with Paul's struggle. The old nature, a slumbering giant within, has the potential to litter the landscape of our lives with the wreckage of failure, lost opportunity, and shattered relationships.

After salvation, each of us carries into the family of God a private, distinct past. It may include unresolved conflicts, addictive behaviors, verbal, physical, or emotional mistreatment. Things we have done may make us want to give up on life.

The good news is we do not have to continue allowing the flesh to rule. We can choose to respond to life through the victory and power of the Holy Spirit.

"Thanks be to God through Jesus Christ our Lord! So then, on the one hand I myself with my mind am serving the law of God, but on the other, with my flesh the law of sin. There is therefore now no condemnation for those who are in Christ Jesus. For the law of the Spirit of life in Christ Jesus has set you free from the law of sin and of death" (Rom. 7:25–8:2).

Our submission to the Holy Spirit is important, not only for our sake, but for others. "For the mind set on the flesh is death, but the mind set on the Spirit is life and peace" (Rom. 8:6). Unfortunately, our mistakes, miscues, and misdeeds—products of sin—often involve the mistreatment of others.

Scripture graphically describes the fruit of the flesh:

Adam and Eve, made in God's image and placed in a perfect environment, sin by disobeying God and eating the forbidden fruit in the Garden of Eden (Gen. 3).

Abraham, a great man of faith and a friend of God, has relations with Hagar instead of waiting for God's provision of a son through relations with his wife, Sarah (Gen. 15–17).

King David, described as a man after God's own heart, pursues an adulterous relationship with Bathsheba and arranges for the death of her husband, Uriah (2 Sam. 11).

Solomon, the wisest man who ever lived, marries foreign wives who worship pagan gods (1 Kings 11).

Ananias and Sapphira, leaders in the early church, lie about the price of their property (Acts 5).

This small sampling reminds us that if we're not aware of the battle within, we will be defeated. Yes, the *power of sin* has been broken by Jesus Christ and the presence of the Holy Spirit in our lives guarantees the potential for victory is there. But living the Christian life is a process. As believers, we CHOOSE to let the *power of God* break fleshly strongholds in our lives. Obedience to God is the only way to be victorious over sin.

THE DEVIL

Satan is a defeated foe, but for now he is alive and well, enjoying his brief moment on earth. And we can be assured he'll throw fiery darts our way as we march toward maturity. This is why David says, "The LORD is my strength and my shield; my heart trusts in him, and I am helped. My heart leaps for joy and I will give thanks to him in song" (Ps. 28:7 NIV).

Scripture refers to him as "...the prince of the power of the air, of the spirit that is now working in the sons of disobedience" (Eph. 2:2).

Satan knows that Jesus has won the ultimate victory over death and he cannot do anything to Him, so his focus is upon God's children on earth.

In the Old Testament Book of Job, we read that Satan went to God and said, "Have you not put a hedge around him and his household and everything he has? You have blessed the work of his hands, so that his flocks and herds are spread throughout the land. But stretch out your hand and strike everything he has, and he will surely curse you to your face" (Job 1:10–11 NIV).

Now Job was a blameless and upright man who feared God and shunned evil. He was the father of seven sons and three daughters. He owned real estate, commercial properties, and a great deal of livestock.

When Satan secured permission to attack Job, the missiles of spiritual warfare started to fly. The Sabeans attacked, killing Job's employees except one who ran home to tell Job that his one thousand oxen and five hundred donkeys were stolen.

When that survivor finished speaking, another servant appeared, breathlessly reporting that lightning had sparked a fire which killed seven thousand sheep and all the other servants. As if that were not enough, a tornado hit the house where all Job's children were gathered. No survivors.

Job dropped to his knees and wailed, "Naked I came from my mother's womb, and naked I will depart. The LORD gave and the LORD has taken away; may the name of the LORD be praised" (Job 1:21 NIV). Job had set his heart to worship God, regardless of the circumstances in his life.

After a brief reprieve, Satan returns. He is firing missiles at Job's physical body, but God tells Satan he cannot kill him. Painful sores erupt from the soles of Job's feet to the top of his head. It gets so bad he uses a piece of pottery to scrape himself as he sits among the ashes.

His wife, with the gift of discouragement, is no help as she responds, "Are you still holding on to your integrity? Curse God and die!" (Job 2:9 NIV). Three so-called friends come to visit and offer pious platitudes instead of true compassion.

You might expect a person under this kind of duress to give up, but the story does not end here. After Job spends some time questioning God, he acknowledges God's sovereignty. Then God restores his riches and his family with even more than he had before.

Satan uses various tactics. Sometimes he just wants us to stay away from fellowship with other believers. While we're alone, he'll help us host our own pity party! He'll also needle us with depression and accuse us of not being a Christian at all. The devil is a shrewd character.

The Lord Jesus warns Simon Peter about him—"Simon, Simon, behold, Satan has demanded permission to sift you like wheat; but I have prayed for you, that your faith may not fail; and you, when once you have turned again, strengthen your brothers" (Luke 22:31–32).

Paul tells the Ephesians to take "up the shield of faith with which we will be able to extinguish all the flaming missiles of the evil one" (Eph. 6:17). But how can we do this?

Neil Anderson, author of *The Bondage Breaker,* insists faith is not mystical. Biblical faith is merely what we believe about God and His Word. He writes, "The more you know about God and His Word, the more faith you will have. The less you know, the smaller your shield will be and the easier it will be for one of Satan's fiery darts to reach its target."[5]

So for a large, protective shield of faith, we must increase our knowledge of God and His Word. Anderson suggests that when Satan bombards us with lies, accusations, and temptations, we should do as Jesus did. Repel Satan's advances with Scripture. We can meet every temptation head-on with true statements about God and with God's Word.

Anderson concludes, "Every time you memorize a Bible verse, listen to a sermon, or participate in a Bible study, you increase your knowledge of God and enlarge your shield of faith."[6]

In addition to enlarging our shield of faith, we can remember the resurrection of Christ. Paul realized that he did not have strength to stand without experiencing "the power of His resurrection" (Phil. 3:10). He wants the unimaginable power that raised Jesus from the dead, flowing through his life. He knows the power of Christ and Christ alone will give him victory over sin and the strength to endure the trials of the day.

"You are from God, little children, and have overcome them; because greater is He who is in you than he who is in the world" (1 John 4:4).

When Satan hurls his arrows at the army of the Lord, we can call upon our Defender, the Lord Jesus Christ. He is greater than the evil one.

Now that we've taken a good look at our enemies, let's get dressed for battle.

CHAPTER FOUR

The War Begins

Prepare your shields, both large and small, and march out for battle!
Harness the horses, mount the steeds! Take your positions with helmets on!
Polish your spears, put on your armor!

JEREMIAH 46:3–4 NIV

Moonlight touched the bedroom walls of a sixty-year-old French schoolmistress. As Madame Angele Levrault opened her eyes, flashes of red and white lights reflected in a mirror across from her bed. The low drone of planes, muffled explosions in the distance, plus the stacatto of flak batteries sent Madame Levrault bounding to the window.

Far up the coast from her small village, brilliant clusters of flares gave the clouds an eerie, red glow. The schoolmistress assumed that Cherbourg, twenty-seven miles away, was being bombed again, but she thought her home was safe. Quickly donning shoes and a robe, she headed through the house and out the back door toward the outhouse.

The garden was peaceful. A combination of moonbeams and flares lit the sky, accentuating long shadows. Within seconds the sound of planes grew louder; they were flying fast and low. A sudden, deafening burst of antiaircraft fire sent Madame Levrault cowering behind a large tree. She was still trembling when the firing stopped abruptly.

As she stepped forward, the silence was broken by a strange fluttering sound. Looking up, Madame Levrault saw a parachute floating toward her garden. Hanging below the chute, silhouetted against the moon, was Private Robert M. Murphy of the 82nd Airborne's 505th Regiment. He hit the ground with a thud and tumbled about twenty yards away. Madame Levrault froze as she watched the eighteen-year-old whip out a knife and cut himself loose from the chute. The tall, slender soldier stood up, laden with weapons and equipment. He spotted the teacher. They gazed at each other for what seemed like an eternity. While the terrified lady watched, he put his finger to his lips, discouraging any sound. Then he swiftly disappeared.

Madame Levrault grabbed her skirts and dashed into her house. She had just witnessed one of the first Americans to land in Normandy at 12:15 A.M., Tuesday, June 6, 1944. D-Day had begun![1]

Before becoming a child of God through faith in Jesus Christ, we are unaware of unseen conflict. However, as strange as it may seem, when we step through the door of salvation into God's Kingdom, our personal war begins. We are the object of enemy attack. Satan's Gestapo tactics include: erecting roadblocks to hinder our fellowship with God, hurling false ideas into our minds, and plotting to steal our peace and joy. How can we fight? What can we do?

Paul answers our questions. Since the apostle encountered many Roman soldiers during his imprisonments, he became familiar with their gear. It seems only natural that he would draw an analogy between the soldier's armor and a Christian's armor. Because spiritual warfare is a reality, Paul wants to make sure we understand all that is involved. He writes: "Finally, be strong in the

Lord, and in the strength of His might. Put on the full armor of God, that you may be able to stand firm against the schemes of the devil. For our struggle is not against flesh and blood, but against the rulers, against the powers, against the world-forces of this darkness, against the spiritual forces of wickedness in the heavenly places. Therefore, take up the full armor of God that you may be able to resist in the evil day, and having done everything to stand firm" (Eph. 6:10–13).

God's strength is our resource during spiritual warfare. He is alive, available, and adequate. That is why Paul calls us to be strong in the Lord and to put on God's full armor because it is necessary in battling against the devil's tricks and devices. Satan plots to defeat and discourage us in our Christian walk, but his strategies are successful only if we go to war unprepared. Now let's get dressed for battle.

THE BELT OF TRUTH

The military girdle is central to the body. Located in the lower abdomen and hips, the loins are regarded as the region of strength. The belt encircles the body. When the soldier girds up his loins, he is ready for action.

In Scripture, truth is manifested in several ways, but it is central to any trusting relationship. God's Word is truth, and God places a high priority on truthfulness. Ananias and Sapphira found this out the hard way in Acts 5. They both lied about a real estate deal and became instant fatalities. Jesus was particularly tough on the scribes and Pharisees for their lack of truthfulness. He called them hypocrites because they tried to appear outwardly clean while their hearts were wicked.

Unlike the Pharisees, truth is displayed in our lives when we stand with personal integrity. "Hold firmly to the truth in love..." (Eph. 4:15 PHILLIPS). "The appropriation of the truth is not intellectual only but moral, expressed through our whole being, in character and action."[2]

An attitude of total truthfulness is consistent with a genuine commitment to Christ. That is why Paul says, "I do my utmost to live my whole life with a clear conscience before God and man" (Acts 24:16 PHILLIPS).

Warren Wiersbe reminds us, "God wants you to be open and honest with Him. Never flatter Him with dishonesty, insincerity, or deception. One way to be honest in your relationship with God is to keep your heart clean. Confess your sins instead of trying to cover them. He knows your heart, so be truthful in your praying."[3]

Jesus Christ, the Living Word, is also truth. Jesus tells his followers, "I am the way, and the truth and the life; no one comes to the Father, but through Me" (John 14:6).

When we go into battle without the belt of truth, our pants fall down. When we are not honest and transparent in our walk with God, our mates, our family, and our accountability brothers and sisters, we have hit the shoulder of the road and are heading toward the ditch. We are opening ourselves up for a real shot from hell.

Living in the realm of the fake and the falsehood will quickly drain and deplete our spiritual resources. We are fighting a losing battle. David writes: "When I kept silent, my bones wasted away through my groaning all day long. For day and night your hand was heavy upon me; my strength was sapped as in the heat of summer. Then I acknowledged my sin to you and did not cover up my iniquity. I said, 'I will confess my transgressions to the Lord'—and you forgave the guilt of my sin" (Ps. 32:3–5 NIV).

David then says: "Surely *you desire truth in the inner parts*, you teach me wisdom in the inmost place" (Ps. 51:6 NIV).

When we come to Christ, the Holy Spirit creates pressure points in our lives that focus on areas that need purifying. Our pride naturally resists this pressure and will try to find solace in denial. When we succumb to this overpowering force in our lives, we find ourselves trafficking in untruthfulness. Satan, the father of lies, is clapping his hands with glee. Another soldier out of commission. Taking the initiative to confess and forsake this lifestyle and come out into the light is the way to deal with this situation (See Ps. 139:23–24, 26:2–3 NIV). "He who conceals his sins does not prosper, but whoever confesses and renounces them finds mercy" (Prov. 28:13 NIV).

Pearl and I have been doing numerous marriage retreats recently. A young couple in attendance had some unresolved secrets between them that had stifled their relationship for seven years. In a flood of emotion and tears these matters were confronted and instantly their sorrow was turned to joy and their mourning into dancing. The love, joy, and peace of their wedding day seventeen years earlier now returned.

What secrets are you holding on to that need resolution? Why risk another day going out without your belt on? You might lose a whole lot more than just your pants!

BREASTPLATE OF RIGHTEOUSNESS

The second piece of armor is the breastplate of righteousness. This is like a bulletproof vest which protects the heart, lungs, and other vital organs. While wearing this breastplate, Satan's fiery darts and accusations will come flying toward us, but we can stand firm. Our heart is protected.

Another way to think of righteousness is—our right standing with God. When we receive Christ as Savior and Lord by faith, we are declared righteous in God's sight.

In contrast, Scripture also speaks of self-righteousness which is the product of our own performance. Isaiah says, "All our righteous acts are like filthy rags" (Isa. 64:6 NIV). This reminds us once again that our human efforts to become right with God always fail. Our only shelter from Satan comes from the righteousness of Christ which we appropriate by faith.

Scripture also speaks of practical righteousness, the changed life we live when Christ indwells us. Paul speaks to the Philippians about, "having been filled with the fruit of righteousness which comes through Jesus Christ, to the glory and praise of God" (Phil. 1:11). This righteousness flows from a life obedient to God's Word. In this case, the quality of our changed lives deflects the devil's bullets of doubt.

The daily experiential knowledge of Christ causes us to be sure of our position in Him. As we strap on the breastplate of righteousness we can say with assurance, "I know whom I have believed and I am convinced that He is able to guard what I have entrusted to Him until that day" (2 Tim. 1:12).

Paul says in 1 Thessalonians 5:8: "But we who are of the day, let us be self-controlled, having clothed ourselves with a breastplate of faith and love, and as a helmet, the hope of salvation." That breastplate protects us from a culture that wants our hearts—a world that wants to squeeze us into its mold.

So many young Christian girls give their hearts to young men who have no desire to serve the Lord and soon they are living in the realm of chaos, compromise and confusion. The same scenario is played out time after time by young men who take their first drag on a marijuana joint. Going out into the world without our vest on can lead us to make some very poor choices.

On the other hand, the breastplate preserves us. Daniel had his breastplate on when he faced a choice about diet: "But Daniel resolved not to defile himself with the royal food and wine, and he asked the chief official for permission not to defile himself this way" (Dan. 1:8 NIV). His request was granted.

When we're not wearing our breastplate we become

chameleons. We're constantly taking our color from the last environment we crawled across. We become thermometers instead of thermostats. Thermometers only register the temperature, thermostats determine it. Peter drew near to warm himself at the fire of the enemy and soon found himself denying his Lord. "Be on the alert, stand firm in the faith, act like men, be strong" (1 Cor. 16:13).

FEET SHOD WITH THE GOSPEL OF PEACE

A good soldier knows the importance of proper footgear. Well-fitting, heavy leather boots with a steel reinforced toe will take us many miles and many hours into battle. On the other hand—blisters, cuts, or twisted ankles put us out of commission before the battle is won—hence, the agony of *de-feet.*

Without the gospel of peace, we will suffer spiritually. So what are our spiritual shoes? How can we assume a steady march with a resolved frame of heart?

We might think about the soles as being the foundational peace we have with God once we have received Christ. "Therefore having been justified by faith, we have peace with God through our Lord Jesus Christ" (Rom. 5:1).

The foam-fitted lining which soothes and protects as we fight on life's daily battlefronts is described in Isaiah. "The fruit of righteousness will be peace; the effect of righteousness will be quietness and confidence forever" (Isa. 32:17 NIV).

The outer leather gives protection and surefooted stability. "Great peace have they who love your law, and nothing can make them stumble" (Ps. 119:165 NIV). This outward peace becomes a guard against the rains, mud, and other realities of trudging in the trenches. "Now may the Lord of peace personally give you his peace at all times and in all ways" (2 Thess. 3:16 PHILLIPS).

The assurance of peace will give us strong support in the

midst of adversity. When our feet are shod with the gospel of peace, we are less likely to be tripped up by Satan's schemes. Trekking the trail in shoes of settled issues gives us great stability and footing from which to wage war. The foundational truths of the gospel provide this for us. Like Martin Luther we can stand saying: "Here I stand, God help me!"

Few have gotten as much flak for their faith as Charles Colson. The press was vicious, Christian brothers and sisters were suspicious, but Chuck knew what had happened in his life.

In his book, *Life Sentence,* he quotes D. L. Moody: "When I was converted, I made this mistake: I thought the battle was already mine, the victory already won, the crown already in my grasp. I thought the old things had passed away, that all things had become new, and that my old, corrupt nature, the old life, was gone. I found out, after serving Christ for a few months, that conversion was only like enlisting in the army—that there was a battle on hand."[4]

When the battle is the hottest and it seems like all hell has broken loose, we can join Isaiah in saying: "Because the Sovereign LORD helps me, I will not be disgraced. Therefore have I set my face like flint, and I know I will not be put to shame" (Isa. 50:7 NIV).

THE SHIELD OF FAITH

The shield in the Roman soldier's attire was about two-and-one-half feet wide and four feet long. It was made of wood and overlaid with linen and leather to absorb fiery arrows.

Paul tells us to take up our shield of faith that we "will be able to extinguish all the flaming missiles of the evil one" (Eph. 6:16).

Here we must not underestimate the power of the enemy. Satan's quiver is loaded with a number of fiery arrows. Here are a few and their descriptions.

ARROWS IN SATAN'S QUIVER:

DOUBT—Satan wants us to doubt God's goodness in the midst of difficult circumstances.

DECEIT—Satan wants to fool us and fake us into following his plan.

DEFENSIVENESS—He delights in seeing us defend ourselves and rationalizing our behavior that is contrary to the desires of the Heavenly Father.

DISCOURAGEMENT—Satan knows if he can get us discouraged, our next step is to throw in the towel and quit trying.

DISTRACTION—He loves to scramble our priorities and get us to invest our time on temporal things rather than eternal matters.

DIVISION—Satan wishes to divide and conquer marriages, families, and churches. Warring factions lose their witness and their joy.

DESTRUCTION—With sovereign permission Satan destroyed Job's business, possessions, and wiped out all ten of his children. He can wreak havoc when he is turned loose. The casualties of war mount with his every effort.

DISOBEDIENCE—Satan has used this one ever since the Garden of Eden to cause the downfall of many believers.

DOCTRINAL ERROR—He tries to inflict false doctrine by using counterfeit ministers and false teachers to pervert the pure teaching of Scripture.

DELAY—Paul tells the Thessalonians that he has been hindered by Satan in coming to see them.

DENIAL—If we fail to face reality, Satan has free reign, and he loves to be in that position.

After examining Satan's arsenal it is easy to understand why we need a shield of faith. But what is it and how can we use it?

Christian faith has three tenses: past, present, and future. The past tense speaks of salvation. "For by grace you have been saved through faith; and that not of yourselves, it is the gift of God" (Eph. 2:8). An eternal transaction took place when we were born by the Holy Spirit into God's family.

Faith's present tense is revealed in many places in Scripture. The patriarch, Abraham, "did not waver in unbelief, but grew strong in faith, giving glory to God" regarding God's promises (Rom. 4:20). Paul instructs the Corinthians to walk by faith and not by sight (2 Cor. 5:7). He also tells the Galatians "the life which I now live in the flesh I live by faith in the Son of God, who loved me, and delivered Himself up for me" (Gal. 2:20).

James tells us to be joyful when we encounter various trials because the testing of our faith produces endurance (James 1:2–3). Peter also tells us that when we are distressed by trials, the proof of our faith, even though tested by fire, will result in praise and honor to Christ (1 Peter 1:6–7). Although our circumstances will be varied, we can be sure that difficulties will come into our lives, and when they do, they become opportunities for us to exercise faith and to triumph in our trust.

The future is in view when Paul charges Timothy to "Fight the good fight of faith; take hold of the eternal life to which you were called" (1 Tim. 6:12). Later in his second letter to Timothy he says, "I have fought the good fight, I have finished the course, I have kept the faith" (2 Tim. 4:7).

The shield of faith stands between us and this arsenal from hell. It is there to protect us from getting wounded. It is our patriot missile to intercept incoming shots that are designed to do damage and destroy.

"The Lord is my strength and my shield; my heart trusts in him, and I am helped. My heart leaps for joy and I will give thanks to him in song" (Ps. 28:7 NIV). "But the Lord is faithful, and He will strengthen and protect you from the evil one" (2 Thess. 3:3).

When a U.S. spacecraft enters earth's atmosphere, the function of the heat shield is of major concern. It protects the astronauts and their vehicle from burning up on the way back to earth. The Psalmist says: "For the LORD God is a sun and shield; the LORD bestows favor and honor; no good thing does he withhold from those whose walk is blameless" (Ps. 84:11 NIV). Let's allow Him to protect us as we keep our shield of faith in place.

HELMET OF SALVATION

The helmet is a life-preserving piece of equipment. The football player, the polo player, the motorcycle rider, and the soldier will all tell you the same thing. "We need a helmet." Loggers, construction workers, and power-company employees see the helmet as an important part of their equipment. It is designed for protection of vital functions in the head, namely the brain.

When I was a child I used to entertain myself on long trips in the car by reading Burma Shave signs. My favorite is:

Don't lose your head
To gain a minute.
You need your head.
Your brains are in it.

If the thought processes are secure from injury, the battle can be waged as planned.

The citadel of function is the mind. Have you ever watched a football player get his bell rung? He doesn't know where he is and what he is doing.

Satan knows that, so his frontal attack is aimed at storming the fortress. When he has control of the nerve center of operation, it is only a matter of time until conduct will follow. Jesus says: "For it is from inside, from men's hearts and minds, that evil thoughts arise—lust, theft, murder, adultery, greed, wickedness, deceit, sensuality, envy, slander, arrogance, and folly! All these evil things come from inside a man and make him unclean!" (Mark 7:21–23, PHILLIPS).

So how can we resist these temptations?

Salvation serves as our security and our hope. "The LORD is my light and my salvation—whom shall I fear? The LORD is the stronghold of my life—of whom shall I be afraid?" (Ps. 27:1 NIV).

The present tense of our salvation in Christ is the daily growth toward Christlikeness. Another name for this process is called sanctification. Paul told the Philippians to work out their own salvation with a reverential fear and trembling. He reminded them that God is the one who was working in them.

God's purpose is for us to be progressively freed from the power of sin.

"Let us cleanse ourselves from all defilement of flesh and spirit, perfecting holiness in the fear of God" (2 Cor. 7:1). One of the steps necessary in this process is to think God's thoughts (Scripture) and to bring our minds under Christ's control.

Without the helmet of salvation, the soldier becomes easy prey for satanic attack. He moves in immediately to entice us to entertain his thoughts, actions, feelings. If we recognize his tactics, we can be on guard and make certain our helmet is in place. Remember, let's not leave home without our hard hats on!

A number of years ago, while serving the Lord at The Firs Camp and Conference Center, we were involved in clearing a heavily wooded area of timber, so that we might build a barn and establish a horse program. We cleared nearly four hundred trees, bulldozed stumps, and built a barn. Every day we wore hard hats as chain saws hummed because limbs were constantly falling. We called them "widow-makers." I remember being hit several times and each time I would tap my headgear and say, "Thank you!"

SWORD OF THE SPIRIT

So far, the soldier is outfitted in armor designed to protect and defend. At last he is given one offensive weapon—a sword.

In the valley of Elah, David tried on Saul's armor and sword and decided they wouldn't cut it (pun intended). So he took his sling and stones and hit Goliath right between the running lights. He did, however, use Goliath's sword to finish the job. "David ran and stood over him. He took hold of the Philistine's sword and drew it from the scabbard. After he killed him, he cut off his head with the sword" (1 Sam. 17:51 NIV). You can get a lot done with a good sword.

Just as the soldier trains hours on the target range while preparing for battle, so the Christian works to master the Word of God. Jesus gave us an example of how to use Scripture against Satan in Matthew 4 when, after fasting for forty days and nights in the wilderness, Satan tempts Jesus to turn the stones into bread. Jesus answered with a Scripture from the Old Testament (Deut. 8:3)—"It is written, 'Man shall not live by bread alone, but on every word that proceeds out of the mouth of GOD'" (Matt. 4:4).

But Satan did not stop with just one temptation, he took Jesus into the holy city and stood Him on the pinnacle of the temple, and said to Him, "If you are the Son of God throw Yourself down." Furthermore, Satan cleverly quoted Scripture from Psalms to indicate the angels would save Jesus (Ps. 91:11–12 NIV). But Jesus countered with the verse, "You shall not tempt the LORD your GOD" (Matt. 4:7; Deut. 6:16).

Did the devil give up? No! A third time he took Jesus to a high mountain and told Him He could have all the kingdoms of the world if He would fall down and worship Satan. Did Jesus give in? No!

Jesus said to him, "Begone, Satan! For it is written, 'You shall worship the LORD your GOD, and serve Him only'" (Matt. 4:10). Then the devil left Jesus alone, and angels ministered to Him.

Often it seems during the times of greatest stress and even during times when we seem to be growing spiritually, Satan tries to tempt us and get us to neglect God's truth. He may offer a half-truth or try to disguise something as good when it is not.

He delights in cluttering our lives with so many demands that we fail to have any time in the Word. Satan knows we may have a great defense, but we will never score without an offense. If he can keep the sword out of our hand, it's a piece of cake to whip us!

I remember in my early ministry how I used to rationalize my study time in the Word for teaching others as adequate for my own soul as well. After getting nailed real good a couple of times, the Lord got my attention. Now my own funeral will be all that breaks my earthly appointment with my heavenly Father. And really that's no big deal since I will have already entered His presence for eternity. I am committed to spending personal quality time in the Word first thing every day. Reading, meditating, and memorizing passages that will make me fruitful as the day unfolds.

DRESSED FOR VICTORY

When do we get dressed for these battles? Every day. One woman I know prays the Ephesians passage for her son each morning before he heads out to school. She mentally dresses him out in his armor and sends him out the door while singing "Onward Christian Soldiers."

Does the Ephesians passage remind us of science fiction or some far-out fairy tale? That's what Satan would like us to believe.

He doesn't want us to know the truth. Now that we do, we'll be ready for him and he won't like it—that's for sure.

Satan's desire is to mentally tie us up and trap us in some kind of bondage. But Satan is no match for our Commander-in-Chief. Jesus has come to set us free. He is greater than Satan.

CHAPTER FIVE

Going Home

For we walk by faith and not by sight—we are of good courage, I say, and prefer rather to be absent from the body and to be at home with the Lord. Therefore also we have as our ambition, whether at home or absent, to be pleasing to Him.

2 CORINTHIANS 5:7–9

The two-story white frame house nestled among sheltering trees as flowers along the walkway announced spring's arrival. Dick's gray hair gleamed in a ray of sunshine as he sat in the front porch swing reading the morning paper. He wondered how much longer he, his wife, Midge, and daughter, Naomi, would be waiting for one of the biggest events of their lives.

Dick's eyes often turned aside from the newspaper to scan the dirt road leading up to the farmhouse. Meanwhile, the tantalizing aroma of homemade bread wafted through the windows as Midge hustled about the kitchen. Twelve-year-old Naomi primped in front of the mirror as though rehearsing for her first date.

Then Dick spotted someone in the distance walking briskly down the path. Could it be? No, probably not. Jimmy was just a boy when he left for military service two years ago. But as the tall, slender image came nearer, Dick noticed the man's clothes. Yes, it was an army uniform.

Dick called to Midge, "Honey, someone's coming. I can't tell who it is, but he's wearing a uniform."

Midge didn't take time to remove her apron as she and Naomi rushed out to the porch. Midge grabbed Dick's hand, held it tightly for a moment, and gasped, "I think it's Jimmy!"

As the young man reached the ninety-degree turn to the house, he broke into a run. The family on the porch simultaneously bolted toward him. They met halfway, screaming, crying, hugging, and rejoicing. Jimmy threw off his backpack, reached down and lifted Naomi into a spin. He kissed and squeezed his mom and hugged his dad.

Tears streamed down Dick's cheeks as he whispered, "I'm so proud of you, son. Welcome home!"

A similar scene must have been repeated many times through the centuries as sons have gone to war, and families have anticipated their return. For the military man, the adrenaline rush of being reunited with loved ones after an extended separation must be greater than the excitement of combat.

To the soldier, going home means his responsibility in the battle is over. Relief and rest are in sight. The Christian experiences a parallel situation. For when our earthly life is ended, our Heavenly Father has prepared a home in heaven which is more beautiful than we could ever imagine. "But just as it is written, 'Things which eye has not seen and ear has not heard, and which have not entered the heart of man, all that GOD has prepared for those who love HIM'" (1 Cor. 2:9).

Many of us have recently become aware of homeless people in many cities throughout the world. As we eat and sleep in our comfortable homes, it is hard to imagine what such a life would be like. However, Billy Graham compares our life on earth to the homeless.

He writes, "In some ways, Christians are homeless. Our true home is waiting for us, prepared by the Lord Jesus Christ. 'Now we know that if the earthly tent we live in is destroyed, we have a building from God, an eternal house in heaven, not built by human hands. Meanwhile we groan, longing to be clothed with our heavenly dwelling' (2 Cor. 5:1–2 NIV). If we look at the beauty He has created on earth, can we even begin to comprehend what He has furnished for us in heaven?"[1]

Without a doubt, heaven is a place designed for us by the greatest architect. Once we're there, we'll stay. But during our lives on earth, we have times when we go away from our homes and return again.

PAINFUL PARTINGS

Pearl and I have experienced a number of painful partings over the years. We parted from our homesteads and moved halfway across the country to begin life together. Over the years we've left places of ministry when called to serve in new endeavors.

Then it was a painful good-bye the last time we visited my dad. As he stood in the yard watching us pull out of his driveway, I had a feeling he would not be on earth much longer. Although he may have felt that, too, he could not seem to verbally express his love for me. Filled with emotion, he just watched in teary silence as we drove away.

A similar emptiness in the pit of my stomach occurred as I drove our daughter's little Ford Ranger pickup loaded with all her belongings to the suburbs of Portland, Oregon. Julea was the last of our five children to leave our Texas nest. I'd planned a parting speech, but was too choked up to say anything. Now a few years later, she's married and capable of making her own decisions. Of course, I'm happy, but sometimes it's hard to believe that my daughter is mature and doesn't need her daddy anymore.

Yes, painful partings are inherent in our lives. However, the longer we live as Christians, the more opportunities we have to observe some who quit before it's time to go home. Scripture is filled with examples of those who ran away from home. In Genesis 3:9, God calls to Adam, "Where are you?" For the first time, we see how sin separates the created and the Creator.

DEPARTING FROM HOME SPIRITUALLY

Through the years, I've observed six factors which characterize, to some degree or another, people who are spiritually away from home and the close relationship they once had with their Heavenly Father.

- *Neglect of spiritual disciplines*—Failure to deepen their relationship with God by omitting Bible reading, Scripture memory, and prayer.
- *Messed up priorities*—Temporary and material things begin taking the place of more lasting relationships and eternal matters.
- *Loss of God-consciousness*—A growing unawareness of His presence, a loss of the sense of His reality.
- *A cold, callous heart toward the things of God.*
- *A refusal to become accountable to others.*
- *A burning interest in living only for today.*

One of the most familiar and gut-wrenching stories Jesus ever told is found in Luke 15, the parable of the prodigal son. Talk about a painful parting.

Two brothers from the same womb? Impossible! The older one is pliable and finds his pleasure in pleasing Pop. The younger one is a rebel and a renegade right out of the chute. His unbroken spirit showed up early in temper tantrums, the terrible twos, and big-time teenage trouble. The song he wanted sung at his funeral was: "I Did It My Way!" The restrictions and restraints of home were just too much to handle any longer, and he had places to go and people to see. "Father, give me the share of the estate that falls to me" (Luke 15:12).

Dad, I want what is going to be mine when they settle your estate. You aren't going to be around much longer, so it's really no big deal to settle with me ahead of time. The dad responds to the selfish request by dividing his wealth between his two sons. The normal reaction of most dads would be to explode and discipline an ungrateful son or even to write him out of the will entirely, but this dad graciously gives the boy what he wants.

Then what happens? "And not many days later, the younger son gathered everything together and went on a journey into a distant country, and there he squandered his estate with loose living" (Luke 15:13). What seemed like happiness turned into hell as the son descended into an undisciplined lifestyle, gratifying his desires for the moment. Pleasure was priority number one!

"Now when he had spent everything, a severe famine occurred in that country, and he began to be in need. And he went and attached himself to one of the citizens of that country, and he sent him into his fields to feed swine. And he was longing to fill his stomach with the pods that the swine were eating, and no one was giving anything to him" (Luke 15:14–16).

Belly up! Belly empty! God's perfect timing is incredible. In an economic crunch, jobs are hard to find. So this young Jewish man once living high on the hog now stoops to feed them and even wants to dine with them. The very act represents the depths of degradation. The mere presence of pigs was a defilement to the Jew. The boy is now learning by bitter experience that the ways of sin are hard. The fun is done. He is alone, stripped of everything. The repo depot got it all: condo, Jaguar, clothes, credit cards—gone!

Then something happened. He came to his senses and began thinking, "How many of my father's hired men have more than enough bread, but I am dying here with hunger! I will get up and go to my father, and will say to him, 'Father, I have sinned against heaven, and in your sight; I am no longer worthy to be called your son; make me as one of your hired men'" (Luke 15:17–19).

THE SON'S REPENTANCE

One of the first requirements for repentance is to face reality—things as they really are. In the midst of his pain the prodigal recognizes his pride. He stops rationalizing. Suddenly he knows he has made some bad choices, and the first one was leaving his father's home. He may be plagued with thoughts such as "You've blown it; it's too late; you've gone too far." But he took a chance and went home.

I am reminded of the words of Jesus to Peter at a critical moment in his life: "Simon, Simon, behold, Satan has demanded permission to sift you like wheat; but I have prayed for you, that your faith may not fail; and you, when once you have turned again, strengthen your brothers" (Luke 22:31–32).

THE FATHER'S RESPONSE

The father's response demonstrates unconditional love and is a picture of the kind of love God, our Heavenly Father, has for us:

He saw him—The dad watched at the window, paced in the doorway, yearned for the return of the boy with a love that kept him looking till he saw his son in the road. So God is looking for the return of all who move away from him.

He was moved with compassion—The father never stopped

loving his son. It was this love that moved the father into action. God never changes. Even when we are selfish, sinful, sorry, senseless sons, God still loves us.

Conditional love depends upon performance. Unconditional love is a no-strings-attached commitment to an imperfect person. God waits, watches, and rewards a son's repentant heart by rushing out to meet him. "But while he was still a long way off, his father saw him, and felt compassion for him, and ran and embraced him, and kissed him" (Luke 15:20).

Under the law, the prodigal's father could have brought his rebellious son to the elders to have him stoned. But this father is moved with compassion and moves toward his son in reconciliation.

"And the son said to him, 'Father, I have sinned against heaven and in your sight; I am no longer worthy to be called your son'" (Luke 15:21). But before he could finish his speech and ask to become an employee, the dad calls for his servants to bring out the best robe, a ring, and sandals. These dramatic actions protect the son from hostilities of people in the town where they lived, but more importantly, it reveals the intent of our Heavenly Father.

He demonstrated acceptance—The robe assures onlookers that the boy has been accepted by his father, the ring is a sign of authority, and the sandals reveal the boy is not a servant, but a cared-for son.

Then to top it off, his dad calls for a feast and a party, a Texas-sized barbecue. Everyone will eat and be merry, for the son who was once considered dead is now alive. The son is reconciled.

Just as the prodigal son's repentance brought blessings, our contrition and brokenness provide fertile soil for restoration of fellowship with the Lord and with other believers. Leaving a disobedient lifestyle reaps many rewards.

Allen (not his real name), a good buddy of mine, went

through a midlife crisis several years ago. Like Solomon in Ecclesiastes, he thought everything in life was meaningless. Losing his spiritual vision and zest for life, he found excuses not to see old friends, he avoided accountability, and began pursuing a different lifestyle. Allen's work offered him more opportunities to travel without his wife, the children were out of the nest, and everything meaningful became superficial, including his time alone with God.

Within months, Allen was immorally involved with another woman, but his wife, like a rock, continued to hang in there. Finally, she confronted him with tough love, forcing him to make a choice. This mandate from his spouse coupled with the verbal assaults from the kids and the pressure of the Spirit of God finally brought Allen to repentance and reconciliation. Now the years have passed and with the coming of grandkids, Allen is thankful the painful parting did not become a reality.

The level of sensitivity and servanthood in their marriage has reached new plateaus. Our fellowship and his friendship with other believers was restored when he finally came to his senses. At one point, some of us were tempted to give up and think he would never change, but now Allen has a new softness and a renewed appreciation for his family.

LIFE NOT ENTIRELY OUR OWN

Perhaps Allen finally realized he does not own himself. God does. When a good soldier joins the military service, his life is under the direction of military authorities. He may be called in the middle of the night or transferred on short notice to another location. He may even be sent for foreign service against his wishes. But he cooperates with his commander.

In a similar way, the Christian man who joins himself to the Lord is one spirit with Him. Scripture says, "Flee immorality.

Every other sin that a man commits is outside the body, but the immoral man sins against his own body. Or, do you not know that your body is a temple of the Holy Spirit who is in you, whom you have from God, and that you are not your own? For you have been bought with a price: therefore glorify God in your body" (1 Cor. 6:18–20).

Being a faithful soldier has fabulous rewards. The soldier not only has assurance in his own heart of a job well done, but if he has been outstanding, he may receive a medal or plaque.

The rewards of total commitment to the Commander-in-Chief may not be as tangible, but they are just as real—both on earth and in heaven. That is why Paul could say, "I shall not be put to shame in anything, but that with all boldness, Christ shall even now, as always, be exalted in my body, whether by life or by death. For to me, to live is Christ, and to die is gain" (Phil. 1:20–21).

THE CHRISTIAN'S HOME

Paul realizes that glorifying Christ is the most important pursuit in his earthly life. Yet he is not afraid to die because he knows his real citizenship is in heaven.

For the believer, going home means eternal life which begins at the time of salvation will extend beyond the earth. Our Heavenly Father is preparing a place for us more beautiful than we could ever imagine. Because Jesus Christ overcame physical death through the Resurrection, we, too, have hope for life beyond the grave.

A story is told of a woman whose eyes were troubling her. After an examination, the oculist told her she needed to rest her eyes by looking out her window to the mountains far away. She found that five or ten minutes each day of looking in the distance rested her eyes.

"She found in the oculist's direction, a parable for her own daily life. 'Soul of mine,' she says to herself, 'are you tired of the little treadmill round of care and worry, of the conflicts with evil, of the struggles after holiness, of the harrowing grief of this world—tired of today's dreary commonplace? Then rest your spiritual eyes by getting a far vision. Look up to the beauty of God's holiness. Look in upon the throngs of the redeemed, waiting inside the gates. Look out upon the wider life that stretches away illimitably.'"[2]

Could our own spiritual vision use a checkup? Going home not only means transferring to a different abode, but more importantly, eternal fellowship with Christ. Jesus said, "In My Father's house are many dwelling places; if it were not so, I would have told you; for I go to prepare a place for you. And if I go and prepare a place for you, I will come again, and receive you to Myself; that where I am, there you may be also" (John 14:2–3).

As Charles Haddon Spurgeon wrote, "Living or dying we are the Lord's. If we live, Jesus will be with us; if we die, we shall be with Jesus."[3]

IT MAY BE LATER THAN YOU THINK

Jean awakened from a deep sleep and realized it was time to meet with her first love, the Lord Jesus. She turned toward Charles, her husband of forty-four years and whispered: "Good morning, sweetheart!"

Later in her quiet time she read, "Come now, you who say, 'Today or tomorrow, we shall go to such and such a city and spend a year there and engage in business and make a profit.' Yet you do not know what your life will be like tomorrow. You are just a vapor that appears for a little while and then vanishes away" (James 4:13–15).

Jean could have endlessly mused about her sixty-seven years.

How good God had been! After leaving Decatur, Texas, she had met Charles at Wheaton College in Illinois. His contagious enthusiasm ignited her life with joy. He meant everything to her.

His tireless energy propelled them as a couple through his training in dental school, five years of medical missionary service in the Belgium Congo, and into his professorship of Dental Radiology at a major university.

As a supportive wife, Jean, also a registered nurse, conscientiously balanced her career with mothering their four daughters. Remembering the death of one infant daughter often brought tears, but Jean remained steadfast in faith throughout life's trials.

As a bold intercessor, Jean often prayed for the lost and dying, especially in India. She prayed for the hill-country pastors whom she and Charles had met four months earlier while visiting the Hindustan Bible Institute.

The morning passed quickly as Charles called Jean to breakfast. They prayed together, ate quickly, and hastily prepared for an engagement to complete the paperwork for their Social Security benefits.

Heavy freeway traffic almost detained them, but they arrived just in time for their 9:00 A.M. appointment on April 19, 1995, at the Alfred P. Murrah Federal Building, Oklahoma City, Oklahoma.

"Welcome home my children.
Your condo and table are ready!"

PART TWO

The Athlete

CHAPTER SIX

Examining the Arena

Again therefore Jesus spoke to them, saying, "I am the light of the world; he who follows Me shall not walk in the darkness, but shall have the light of life.

JOHN 8:12

Wow! You've got to be kidding!" I yelled. "Three tickets to watch the Cowboys play the Chiefs on Thanksgiving day? Hey! that's tomorrow and we're supposed to eat Thanksgiving dinner at your house."

As I chatted with my son-in-law, Mark, we both knew the guys in our family wanted to use those tickets. But—how? We had a logistical problem. Mark had the tickets but he lives over one hundred miles from Texas Stadium.

So negotiations began with my daughter, Becky, and husband, Ray, who live in Las Colinas, only five minutes from Texas Stadium. Could we? Would we? Yes! We threw the turkey and trimmings in the car early the next morning and headed toward Big D.

Following our fabulous Thanksgiving dinner at Becky and Ray's, Mother and her two daughters stayed at the house for a hen party while Dad and two sons-in-law headed out to the game.

I was so excited! We arrived an hour and a half before kick-off. Then as the players did calisthenics and sprinted during their practice drills, I began to realize something. We miss most of the pregame activity when watching the games on TV. During the preliminaries the athletes warm up, throw passes, and get the feel of the turf.

Serious competitors, regardless of the event, examine their territory before the real action begins. Ice skaters glide on the ice, skiers race the downhill course, basketball players dribble the gym and shoot baskets. Besides the benefits of physical conditioning, on-site preparation sharpens mental alertness. Knowing the eccentricities of the playing field may mean the difference between the athlete's victory or defeat.

In a similar way, Christians benefit from examining the culture in which we live. Christians have always lived in societies which were generally antagonistic to biblical beliefs. However, in modern America the trend toward outright hostility is increasing.

Jim Black, in his book *When Nations Die*, makes ten observations about the United States today which portray social, cultural, and spiritual symptoms of danger ahead:

1. General increase in lawlessness throughout the culture
2. The loss of economic discipline and self-restraint
3. A decline in the quality and relevance of education
4. Rising bureaucracy, government regulation, and taxes
5. A weakening of the foundational principles that contributed to the greatness of the nation
6. A loss of respect for established religions
7. Increase in materialism
8. A rise in immorality
9. The lure of alien gods
10. A decline in the value of human life.[1]

Some practical ways these trends are revealed can be noted in our daily newspapers. Stories about:

Militant radical feminists
Gay-rights advocates who justify their sin
People who are outraged that a mother drowns her two sons, but who support another woman's rights to kill her unborn child
A justice system that too often rules in favor of the criminal and forgets the victims and their families
Policemen who go to war when they leave for work
High school graduates needing remedial reading classes
TV channels filled with violence, murder, sex, drugs, profanity, nudity, and dysfunctional families

Another tragedy of America is that many have replaced God-given initiative with selfish entitlement. "In God We Trust" may still be inscribed on our coins but "Me First" is engraved upon our hearts. We crave our rights, and selfishness consumes us like a cancer.

As a nation, the further we slip away from God and His Word, the more everyone does what is right in his own eyes. However, the recent emphasis upon biblical family values and other trends reveal that America still has *heart*. Hopefully this new conservatism will prove to be more than a promising blip on the nation's otherwise flat moral EKG.

How is a Christian to live in this kind of world? How can we impact our society in a positive way? What can we do or say to make a difference for Christ? Eric Liddell gives us some clues.

THE LEGACY OF ERIC LIDDELL

One of the most amazing men of all times was labeled "Scotland's Greatest Athlete," and his story is featured in the film *Chariots of*

Fire. Eric Liddell lived from 1902–1945, and his athletic accomplishments included a British record in the 100-yard dash that stood for thirty-five years. At the 1924 Olympics he refused to run in the 100-meter race, his strongest event. Why? Because the qualifying heats were held on a Sunday. But later in the week he participated in the 200-meter race, winning a bronze medal, and he set a world record in the 400-meter race.

Eric Liddell was known as a man whose supreme goal was to know and to obey Christ. He challenged others to be Christlike in character, at home, at work, and in social life—an ideal not merely to be admired, but to be followed.

When Eric's daughter was asked by a *Decision* magazine representative to recall a word of wisdom that her father told her, she thought of a footrace in which she did not run her fastest:

"I remember my father saying to me, 'Now, Tricia, when you're striving for something, you strive for the best. You don't just fool around with your energies and talents. You always strive for the very best in yourself.'"[2]

Eric Liddell's life seems to magnify four characteristics of a man who stood for Christ, no matter what. These qualities—Conviction, Character, Courage, and Christianity—were also seen in many of America's founding fathers. We need more men like them today.

CONVICTION

Men and women of real conviction face the challenges of living life to the fullest on the basis of what they know to be right. They purposefully confront the pressures of a society which would rather choose conformity than righteousness. The Old Testament character Daniel and his friends are such men.

Daniel's story is fascinating. As a Jewish youth living in Judah, he and three other good-looking, intelligent guys are captured by the officials of King Nebuchadnezzar of Babylon when his men seize Jerusalem. The king wants some young men who are sons of nobility to learn the pagan language and customs and then be assigned as his personal attendants.

The four young men are given new names and the king chooses a menu for them which includes the king's favorite rich foods and wine. But Daniel and his friends make a special request of the official commander and ask, "Please test your servants for ten days: Give us nothing but vegetables to eat and water to drink. Then compare our appearance with that of the young men who eat the royal food, and treat your servants in accordance with what you see" (Dan. 1:12).

At first the commander doesn't want to listen. He's afraid he'll forfeit his head to the king. But God grants Daniel favor in the eyes of the commander and he agrees to Daniel's plan.

After ten days, Daniel and his friends are noticeably more healthy than all the youths who have been eating the king's choice food. So the commander allows them to continue. After the allotted time, they are chosen for the king's personal service. In the meantime, God is giving them knowledge, discernment, and wisdom. Daniel is assigned to the king's court while his friends are designated as administrators in Babylon.

Then comes the real test for Daniel's friends. Nebuchadnezzar sets up a golden image and commands everyone in Babylon to fall down and worship the idol. The king says, "Whoever does not fall down and worship will immediately be thrown into a blazing furnace."

The young men only worship the one true God. They stand firm in their conviction and while everyone else falls to their knees and bows to the golden image, Shadrach, Meshach, and Abed-nego refuse. Their lack of compliance is reported to the king.

Enraged, the king brings the men into his chamber and commands them to bow down to the golden image. He is furious as he shouts, "...what god will be able to rescue you from my hand?"

Steadfast in their convictions, the three men do not move. They tell Nebuchadnezzar, "If we are thrown into the blazing furnace, the God we serve is able to save us from it, and he will rescue us from your hand, O king. But even if he does not, we want you to know, O king, that we will not serve your gods or worship the image of gold you have set up."

Nebuchadnezzar is livid. In his wrath he orders his servants to "heat the furnace seven times hotter than usual."

The military do their job. Shadrach, Meshach, and Abed-nego are tied up in their trousers, their coats, their caps, and other clothes and cast into the midst of the blazing furnace. The fire is so hot, the men who throw them in are burned to death, but the king stands up astounded as he asks, "Weren't there three men that we tied up and threw into the fire?"

The officials answer, "Certainly, O king."

The king exclaims, "Look! I see four men walking around in the fire, unbound and unharmed, and the fourth looks like a son of the gods."

Then Nebuchadnezzar comes to the door of the furnace and commands them to come out. To the amazement of the king and all the officials, the men walk out unharmed, their clothes not burned, their hair not singed, nor do they smell like fire.

The king responds and says, "Praise be to the God of Shadrach, Meshach, and Abed-nego, who has sent his angel and rescued his servants! They trusted in him and defied the king's command and were willing to give up their lives rather than serve or worship any god except their own God."

He continues, "Therefore I decree that the people of any

nation or language who say anything against the God of Shadrach, Meshach and Abed-nego be cut into pieces and their houses be turned into piles of rubble, for no other god can save in this way."

Then the king caused the three men to prosper in the province of Babylon. (For the complete story read the book of Daniel, chapters 1–6.) Paul enlarges upon the Old Testament account by writing in the New Testament, "And do not be conformed to this world, but be transformed by the renewing of your mind, that you may prove what the will of God is, that which is good and acceptable and perfect" (Rom. 12:2).

Another translator says, "Don't let the world around you squeeze you into its own mould" (PHILLIPS). This is true conviction. In twentieth-century America, we need men and women who are willing to impact our world for Christ simply by standing firm and not conforming to the pressures of society.

CHARACTER

Character is developed by our convictions. What we believe determines what we will do. Abraham Lincoln said, "Character is like a tree and reputation like its shadow. The shadow is what we think of it; the tree is the real thing."[3] Character is manifested by what we think, say, and do. It is who we are in the dark when no one can see.

The founding fathers realized the strength of a nation lies in the character of its citizens. However, through the years we can see how our children reflect our lack of a moral national compass.

In a message entitled "America, You're Too Young to Die," given on July 5, 1992, David T. Moore reported that in 1960, 53 percent of American teenagers had never been kissed. More than half had never "necked." Over 30 percent were virgins. By 1990, the numbers had shifted dramatically.

- One in five teenagers loses his or her virginity before the age of thirteen.
- Nineteen percent of American teenagers have had more than four sexual partners before high school graduation.
- Each day 2,795 students get pregnant, 1100 get abortions, 1200 give birth.
- Each day another 623 contract STDs (sexually transmitted diseases).
- AIDS infection among high school students is up 700 percent from two years ago.[4]

Statistics cited by former U.S. Secretary of Education and anti-drug czar William J. Bennett tend to support Moore's findings. Bennett quotes a Children's Defense Fund claim that a baby is born to a teenage mother every 64 seconds in this country. Approximately 40 percent of teen pregnancies, about 400,000 per year, end in abortion.[5]

Sexual promiscuity is not our only problem. David T. Moore contends that 3.3 million problem drinkers and 500,000 alcoholics are present on our high school campuses. On any given weekend in America, 30 percent of the student population is drunk.[6]

It's tough to be a kid at home, too. Every year over one million American children have parents who separate or divorce. Approximately half of all marriages in America can be expected to end in divorce.[7]

In professional sports, character and personal integrity used to be the vital ingredients necessary for developing a great athlete. Today conviction, character, and commitment have been replaced with "What am I going to get before I let you come and see me play?" You pay and we'll play!

Good news! Before we become too discouraged, not everyone has succumbed to the darkness. Even with the surrounding degradation, men of character are still shining lights. Included in the list are Tom Landry, Joe Gibbs, Steve Largent, Tommy Maxwell, Corey Pavin and Paul Azinger, just to mention a few. They are stalwart men of faith who stand on and live by Christian principles.

COURAGE

Courage is an outgrowth of strong convictions and an evidence of good character. Scripture offers examples of courageous men and women, among them is Gideon, an Israelite, empowered by the Holy Spirit and chosen to deliver Israel from the Baal-worshiping Midianites. The Lord directs Gideon. From an army of ten thousand he chooses three hundred men. They will be pitted against armies of the Midianites and Amalekites which are as numerous as the sand on the seashore.

Even before the attack begins, a man relates a dream to Gideon in which God has given the camp of Midian into his hands. In faith, Gideon divides his three hundred men into three companies of one hundred each. He gives each man a trumpet and an empty pitcher with a torch inside.

Then Gideon instructs them, "Watch me. Follow my lead. When I get to the edge of the camp, do exactly as I do. When I and all who are with me blow our trumpets, then from all around the camp blow yours and shout, 'For the Lord and for Gideon.'"

So Gideon and his one hundred men arrive at the outskirts of the camp, blow their trumpets, and smash the pitchers in their hands. When three hundred trumpets blast along with the breaking glass and torches, the Midianites are terrified. In their God-ordained confusion, they turn their swords upon one another, fighting and fleeing.

Thus, the Lord gives Midian into the hands of Gideon and his three hundred men as they courageously follow the Lord's unconventional instructions and reap the reward. (For the entire story, read Judges 7–8.)

An inspiring modern example of courage is Dave Dravecky, a major-league baseball player who developed cancer in his pitching arm. The San Francisco Giants' pitcher persevered through the long process of surgery and rehabilitation. He made an amazing comeback and pitched again. Unfortunately, his arm could not bear the strain and it broke. Dave's arm was eventually amputated and his baseball career was over. Although the trauma has taken its emotional toll on Dave and his wife, Janice, they have remained firm in their Christian testimony.

In March, 1990, Dravecky, his wife, and two children were called to the White House where Dave received the American Cancer Society's Courage Award.[8] In the midst of adversity, Dave Dravecky continues to impact the lives of others through his testimony shared in both of his books, *Comeback* and *When You Can't Come Back*.

Another athlete, Wally Frost, played on the Wheaton College football team in 1946. At 6'4" 235 pounds, he was a natural and one of only two freshmen to make the varsity team. He earned the starting tackle position.

But one afternoon following practice, everything changed. Wally noticed a tingling sensation in his legs, along with a headache and burning fever. He was ordered to bed, and within a few days, the creeping paralysis of polio claimed the legs that had run the football field so many times.

"It was completely devastating to me at first," he remembers. "I would pray to God that I would go to sleep and not wake up."

Even though he was a Christian, sports had become the focus of Wally's life. More than anything, he wanted to become a professional football player. But when wheelchair confinement rearranged his life, Wally did not give up. He changed his priorities.

The Lord brought a young, bubbly nursing student into his life who soon discovered Wally had a special place in her heart. They eventually married and despite the doctor's prediction that they could not have children, Wally proved him wrong five times.

From his wheelchair, Wally spent endless hours hitting grounders and roughhousing with his children, all of whom engaged in their own athletic activities—especially Wally's son Dave, who became a pitcher for the California Angels.

Wally coupled his excitement about the Christian faith with his love for young people. He served more than twenty-five years as a college academic counselor where he repeatedly convinced students that someone cared.

Was Wally handicapped? Not in the eyes of his family and those who knew him. He was a courageous man who loved the Lord and spent eight hours a day working, eight hours a day sleeping, and eight hours being a father.[9]

Another athlete, Dennis Byrd, broke his neck on a Sunday afternoon while playing for the New York Jets against the Kansas City Chiefs. Dennis has written his story in the book *Rise and Walk*. In it he describes how God, grit, and gratitude bring about an incredible series of uplifting incidents. We see courage in a man who just keeps hanging in there!

CHRISTIANITY

The founders of our nation were, by and large, Christian men. David T. Moore maintains that fifty-two of fifty-five signers of the Declaration of Independence were orthodox believers in Jesus Christ.[10]

George Washington established Thanksgiving as a national

holiday to encourage the people to acknowledge with grateful hearts the care, protection, and favors of Almighty God.[11]

Ben Franklin—statesman, philosopher, intellectual—also humbly acknowledged the supremacy of One mightier than man. He often quoted Psalm 127:1, "Unless the Lord builds the house, its builders labor in vain" (NIV).

Abraham Lincoln, like Franklin, also encouraged prayer prior to business and encouraged his audience to "recognize the sublime truth (announced in Holy Scriptures and proven by all history), that those nations only are blessed whose God is the Lord."[12]

What can we do today to let our light shine? We can begin in our own hearts and homes to develop the character qualities described in Scripture that will help us become stronger witnesses for Christ in our individual arenas.

Bob Briner has written three books that have really pushed my button: *Roaring Lambs, Squeeze Play,* and *Lambs Among Wolves*. His call is to confront this culture by bringing Christ into the media, theater, athletics, and arts. No matter where we work or what kind of tasks we perform, we can let our light shine by submitting to the authority of Christ in our lives.

We need to constantly remind ourselves that we are playing this game of life on the road. Satan has the home-field advantage. However, as children of the King, we have the winning game plan.

Chapter Seven

Training for Success

Discipline yourself for the purpose of godliness.

1 Timothy 4:7

In the sizzling Texas heat, long before cool nights set autumn leaves ablaze with color, the Dallas Cowboys travel to Austin, Texas for training camp. There the guys exercise, run plays, engage in conditioning, studying, and preparation for the football season. The coach formulates his idea of a winning team, and they start the season with a perfect record like everyone else until they play their first game.

Will the discipline pay off? Each team playing in the league has the privilege of participating, but only one will win the contest. As the season comes to a close, only one team wins the Superbowl.

When Tom Landry was still coaching, he invited me to speak at a Dallas Cowboys playoff game chapel service where I asked the question, "Is big-time athletics in the United States degenerating from commitment to a contract?" Looking back now, my comments seem prophetic.

Fortunately, Christians aren't competing with one another for a single prize, but we are committed to finishing well. Living the Christian life is not a game to be enjoyed, but rather a challenge to fully accomplish the Father's purpose for our lives, no matter what. Unlike some athletes today, a child of God does not go on strike.

The passion to become all that God wants us to be fuels the fire that keeps us going. Fourth and long with seconds on the clock means there's still time for at least one more play. Don't give up. As the old saying goes, "The race is not always to the swift but to those who keep on running."

DISCIPLINE

The key to effective Christian commitment is through the discipline of the total life. Discipline penetrates the spiritual, physical, social, mental, and emotional parts of a person. Show me a man who walks with God, and I'll show you a disciplined individual.

Discipline and discipleship go hand in hand. Walter A. Henrichsen, in his book *Disciples Are Made, Not Born,* writes, "A disciple is a disciplined person. Such a life is not easy, but God never promised us it would be. That it is not easy is clearly seen by the fact that there are so few faithful people around today. The kind of person God uses is the one who has resolved in his soul to stay with it until he accomplishes it."[1]

Oswald Chambers observes, "The great stumbling block in the way of some people being simple disciples is that they are gifted, so gifted they won't trust God. So clear away all those things from the thought of discipleship; we all have absolutely equal privileges, and there is no limit to what God can do in and through us."[2]

He adds, "Being a disciple is to be something that is an infinite satisfaction to Jesus every minute, whether in secret or in public."[3]

It is said of Jesus, He "kept increasing in wisdom and stature, and in favor with God and men" (Luke 2:52). Jesus was human as well as divine. He matured mentally, physically, spiritually, and relationally as a direct result of discipline.

The following questions may serve as a gauge to evaluate the discipline in your life:

1. What is the authority structure in your life? To whom are you responsible?
2. Who are your accountability friends?
3. Where does your career fit into your list of priorities?
4. What plans do you have for deepening your commitment to your marriage partner?
5. What plans do you have to fulfill your parenting responsibilities?
6. What spiritual disciplines are you presently exercising: Bible reading, prayer, scripture memory, devotional reading?

I can hear you saying, "Anderson, it would take a thirty-hour day to get all that done!" I hear you. Realize that as your responsibilities shift with time, some demands will decrease, others will change.

Pearl and I are now enjoying the fruit of our labor in parenting five children and in strengthening our marriage. We haven't stopped working in these areas, but as our children have grown, the large chunks of time once demanded in caring for them are now freed for pursuit of other interests.

I'm not suggesting that a disciplined life is easy, but rewards await the faithful. When I was training for my first marathon, knee and Achilles-tendon injuries kept me limping all the time. I wondered if I'd be able to complete the twenty-six miles. After endless, consistent days of training, I entered the race and finished. It was exhilarating!

Those of us who work out physically usually do so at a set

time and follow a specific routine or schedule. Something similar needs to happen if we want to reach our stride spiritually.

Physical discipline is one thing and spiritual discipline another. For a number of years, I have been faithful to work at Scripture memorization daily, with review, review, review. Recently, I had the joyous experience of quoting verse after verse when I was being grilled by the crowd at a couples' conference during a question-and-answer session. It is a thrill to have the Spirit of God call up verses that are perfect for a situation.

The older I get the harder it is to memorize. The other morning I was having an especially difficult time with some verses and was about ready to quit when I found Psalm 45:1: "My heart is stirred by a noble theme as I recite my verses for the king; my tongue is the pen of a skillful writer" (NIV). Just think, I'm going to get to recite my verses for the King someday! Talk about fresh motivation. Light my fire!

My point is, the rewards came because I was disciplined enough to keep at the task. I would not have finished the marathon, nor could I recall Bible verses from memory if I had not been willing to work at it.

In the New Testament, James speaks of rewards—the crown of life—and Peter speaks of the crown of glory. Paul mentions several crowns in his epistles, including the crown of righteousness: "Henceforth there is laid up for me a crown of righteousness, which the Lord, the righteous judge, shall give me at that day: and not to me only, but unto all them also that love his appearing" (2 Tim. 4:8 KJV).

In our day of *instant* and *easy* we sometimes forget that no man accomplishes much without discipline. I'm sure the apostle Paul was a tremendous sports fan, perhaps an athlete himself. He uses running and fighting analogies often in his writings. Marathons become metaphors for the Christian life.

Just as physical fitness has rules, so does spiritual fitness. As Paul later writes to his protégé, Timothy, "For bodily discipline is only little profit, but godliness is profitable for all things, since it holds promise for the present life and also for the life to come" (1 Tim. 4:8).

OUR PERSONAL TRAINERS

Even if we recognize our need for spiritual discipline, we may quickly ask—But who will help me? For the Christian, our trainers are the three members of the Trinity and they're always available.

First, the Heavenly Father is eager for us to feast at his table. Spiritual nutrition is essential. We are what we eat. Why not be feasting on His Word? Read the Bible carefully and regularly. Pray. And don't forget to savor the cake and ice cream by meditating and memorizing His Word.

Staying in fellowship with the Father keeps us from deceiving ourselves into thinking we are something we are not. It can be like hearing the truth from a doctor.

Dr. Kenneth Cooper of the world-renowned Cooper Aerobics Center in Dallas told a good friend of mine, "You are in great shape for a guy 6'4", but your problem is you're only 5'10"."

God's Word gives us an accurate evaluation of who we are. We cannot fool God. He knows all about us. Through studying His Word we find out more about Him and His purpose for our lives.

The writer of the Book of Hebrews tells his readers that: "For the word of God is living and active and sharper than any two-edged sword, and piercing as far as the division of soul and spirit, of both joints and marrow, and able to judge the thoughts and intentions of the heart" (Heb. 4:12).

The Father does His surgery in our lives by our exposure to His Word. So come on, let's get up on the operating table with the prayer of David on our lips: "Test me, O LORD, and try me, examine my heart and my mind; for your love is ever before me, and I walk continually in your truth" (Ps. 26:2–3 NIV).

Unfortunately, some athletes view God as a trinket or good-luck charm. They think if they go to chapel just before the game, God will see them there and they'll get their wish of hitting the winning home run in the ninth inning or throwing the touchdown pass in the last second to win the ball game. These concepts of God are superstitious and disrespectful.

In the same way, if we desire God for what He might do for us, we miss the reason for fellowship—that we may know Him. Just as sin kept Adam hiding from God, we sometimes want to hide, too. The discipline of confessing our sin and experiencing the cleansing of Christ will help us seek the Father's face instead of running away. Paul tells the leadership in Ephesus: "And now I commend you to God and to the word of His grace, which is able to build you up and to give you the inheritance among all those who are sanctified" (Acts 20:32).

The Holy Spirit is the living water. Jesus said in John 7:38–39: "He who believes in Me, as the Scripture said, 'From his innermost being shall flow rivers of living water.' But this He spoke of the Spirit, whom those who believed in Him were to receive; for the Spirit was not yet given, because Jesus was not yet glorified."

Exercise increases our need for liquids. When running or cycling, I lose quarts of water. I'm like a cracked pot or a leaky vessel. When your radiator leaks you can't go far without heating up. I know I'm that way spiritually, too. When I've been traveling and teaching for days on end, my liquid level gets low. Continuing to run about three quarts low will bring on spiritual burnout quicker than my precious bride Pearl can smell books on my breath. (She is aware that I'm a bookaholic, and she knows every time I darken the door of a bookstore.)

The Holy Spirit is our replenisher. He helps us identify points of resistance so we can confess them. Paul warns the Ephesians by saying: "And do not grieve the Holy Spirit of God, by whom you were sealed for the day of redemption" (Eph. 4:30). We grieve the Spirit when we refuse the washing of the water of the word applied by the Spirit. He grieves when we stay dirty!

Paul warns the Thessalonians by saying: "Do not quench the Spirit" (1 Thess. 5:19). Stop turning off the faucet of the Spirit by your resistance as He is refreshing and refueling you.

Paul commands the Galatians to "Walk by the Spirit, and you will not carry out the desire of the flesh" (Gal. 5:16). Deepen your dependence upon Him in your daily walk.

When the coach begins to see his patterns being played out on the field by the young athletes, he speaks words of encouragement and affirmation that every athlete treasures. Likewise, when we obey the promptings of the Holy Spirit, we also feel a surge of joy. While we may not understand the entire game plan, our responsibility is to do what the Holy Spirit is leading us to do now. Obedience brings joy.

Jesus himself is the third trainer, our model. Most athletes have someone they look up to and admire as they begin their careers. Jesus is not only with us in every situation, He is our hero. He has played the game and survived the conflict—not only survived but soared to victory. He's been through it all. No matter what life throws at us He's been there before. No wonder the writer of Hebrews tells us: "Keep your eyes on Jesus, who both began and finished this race we're in. Study how he did it. Because He never lost sight of where He was headed—that exhilarating finish in and with God—He could put up with anything along the way: cross, shame, whatever. And now He's there, in the place of honor, sitting at the right hand of God the Father. When you find yourselves flagging in your faith, go over that story again, item by item, that long litany of hostility He plowed through. That will shoot adrenaline into your souls" (Heb. 12:2–3 THE MESSAGE).

How comforting to know that Christ is always with us. One day when I was running a long and difficult course, I told the Jewish friend beside me, "I feel like I'm pounding the pavement between two Jews." And I was.

Jesus is always with us—when we work out at the gym, he is there. When we run, he keeps in step with us. He also points the way. Through Scripture, He teaches us winning attitudes and actions. He will be generous with His approval when our race is done!

SETTING GOALS

Along with discipline, setting goals will enable us to grow. Paul knows that he has not yet arrived in his Christian experience. His conversion was only the beginning of his spiritual pilgrimage, not the end. He states, "I press on in order that I may lay hold of that for which also I was laid hold of by Christ Jesus" (Phil. 3:12).

We might think of Paul as a football player—a wide receiver pursuing the pass pattern in order to make the catch. Or perhaps he is like the defensive tackle pursuing the ball carrier in order to make the critical stop.

Having a passionate desire to fulfill the Father's will, I direct all my energies in that effort. I am sustained by three passages of scripture. All of them are in Proverbs.

"Trust in the LORD with all your heart and lean not on your own understanding; in all your ways acknowledge him, and he will make your paths straight" (Prov. 3:5–6 NIV).

"In his heart a man plans his course, but the LORD determines his steps" (Prov. 16:9 NIV).

"Many are the plans in a man's heart, but it is the LORD's purpose that prevails" (Prov. 19:21 NIV).

Setting goals is not a way of telling God what He can and cannot do in our lives. We're not telling Him to sit in the bleachers while we play the game. Rather, goalsetting is a method of taking temporal control of our lives, realizing God is ultimately in charge. It means we're directing our lives toward things He values, realizing that He always has the last word. We can take nothing out of God's sovereign hands.

Dreams are our creative visions of life in the future. We can dream of becoming more and more Christlike, but goals are the specific steps we take to make it happen. While on earth we will always be *becomers*.

Denis Waitley writes, "Dreams and goals should be just out of your present reach but not out of sight. Two great tragedies in life are never to have had great dreams and goals for yourself and to have fully reached them so that tomorrow holds no eager anticipation of challenge."[4]

What greater aim could we have than to become Christlike? If this is our goal, then we mature as doers of the Word, not hearers only. If we just hear an occasional sermon but do not spend time personally with the Heavenly Father, the preacher's words may soon be forgotten. Our response to life situations remains the same. But if we obey by setting goals and following through, we begin to change.

When a man is satisfied with what he has attained, at that moment he ceases to grow. If he thinks he has arrived, he hasn't. The challenge of each day on our spiritual journey is to "grow in the grace and knowledge of our Lord and Savior, Jesus Christ" (2 Pet. 3:18).

I must confess that early in my Christian life my walk with God was a very personal thing. Goal setting, accountability, mentoring, and discipleship were foreign concepts. As a result, I had to learn the hard way not to play the blame game, to get off my self-made pedestal, and to recognize I could not be a Lone Ranger in the Christian life. When I adopted a teachable spirit, I no longer had to rationalize and live in denial. The sheer joy, freedom, and encouragement I've found in developing goals and pursuing accountability friendships makes me sad that I didn't start earlier. I have a large number of these kinds of relationships now and am ready for more!

Six areas which commonly come under scrutiny when setting goals and establishing accountability are:

1. Spiritual Goals—Here we are determining a structure for our daily meeting with the Lord through Bible reading, prayer, scripture memory, and reading the devotional classics. Also included are our goals for ministry. The three E's—Edification, Equipping, and Evangelism—church relationships, spiritual gifts, and ministry to those who need the Savior.

2. Marriage Goals—With our mates we plan the year and set goals for quality time together. Taking time to be together is crucial for a growing relationship. Pearl and I schedule a couple of outings each year just to be away for several days to read, rest, and rejoice in our Lord and each other. Pearl is like my American Express card. I don't leave home without her! By the way, one of your greatest accountability resources is your sweetheart. Talk about somebody who knows you and sees you and can hold your fat to the fire. Let her!

3. Family Goals—These goals continually change as we move from parenting to grandparenting. What do we want to accomplish in our family? Do we have a mission statement? When and where do we go on family vacations? If we don't plan it, it won't happen.

4. Career Goals—What am I doing? Where am I going? When will I know I'm successful? How can I plan now so that I will be able to serve the Lord full-time during the final years of my life?

5. Physical Fitness Goals—What kind of exercise? How often? When? Diet and weight loss are part of this too!

6. Hobbies Goals—Golf? Fishing? Hunting? Reading? How much time?

Once all of this initial work is done, it is then time to share these with our accountability person. Structuring a regular checkup time is necessary to keep us focused.

If we aim at nothing, we hit it every time. Following through on this project will help us draw closer and grow stronger in the Lord.

Dick Flaten, pastor of a dynamic, growing church, has been an inspiration to thousands. After being stricken with cancer, he just kept going. When he was no longer able to continue his pastorate, he stepped into a Bible teaching ministry. Forever etched in my mind are the words he spoke to me at a crucial time in my life. "Don, I'll see you at the finish line."

Paul, in that highly emotional farewell to the Ephesian elders in Acts 20, says much the same thing that Dick had said to me: "But I do not consider my life of any account as dear to myself, in order that I may finish my course, and the ministry which I received from the Lord Jesus, to testify solemnly of the gospel of the grace of God" (Acts 20:24). "And now I commend you to God and to the word of His grace, which is able to build you up and to give you the inheritance among all those who are sanctified" (Acts 20:32). May your tombstone read: "Forgiven! Faithful! Fruitful! Finisher!"

CHAPTER EIGHT

Going for the Gold

I have fought the good fight, I have finished the course, I have kept the faith.

2 TIMOTHY 4:7

During the 1996 summer Olympic games, 4'8" Kerri Strug leaped to her place in history. The eighteen-year-old gymnast and three other U.S. team members were competing with the Russians for first place. Scores were close. The Georgia Dome vibrated and echoed with thirty-two thousand screaming fans. Could the young team meet the challenge?

The Americans had edged ahead on several events: the uneven parallel bars, the balance beam, and the floor routines. But during the last event, the vault, a hush of anticipation stilled the crowd. One U.S. team member ended her attempts by sprawling on the mat both times. Suspense intensified when Kerri, the last team member, stepped up for her turn. It, too, ended in a nasty fall. She rolled over on her ankle and felt a snap. When she stood up, she shook her leg and disappointedly hobbled toward her coach. She was in obvious pain, but her team encouraged her to try again, not realizing her injury was serious. Believing that the gold was at stake, she chose to vault again.

While standing on the end of the runway, Kerri whispered a quick prayer for help. Then she proceeded to run, flip, turn, and soar smoothly, gracefully landing on both feet long enough to score 9.837 before collapsing in pain. The crowd stood—cheering, clapping, some even weeping—in honor of Kerri's outstanding performance. Her gutsy move guaranteed the first gold medal ever won by a U.S. Olympic women's gymnastics team.

Medics rushed to care for Kerri. They wanted to whisk her away to the hospital, but her coach, Bela Karolyi, refused. Instead, he scooped her up into his arms and carried her to the podium. There she and her teammates accepted the rewards they had earned. With tears rolling down her cheeks, in the midst of joy, pain, exhaustion, and exuberance, Kerri Strug received her gold medal. While listening to the national anthem, an audience of thousands observed a dedicated athlete who, despite her agony, did not quit.

Kerri's coach came to her aid in her time of need. As Christians we sometimes fall, but God does not forsake us. Nor does He abandon us during our suffering and affliction. Rather, He puts His arm around us and helps us keep moving toward the goal. Sometimes He carries us, too.

The goal of a Christian is to finish well and to hear the Lord say, "Well done, Thou good and faithful servant" (Matt. 25:21 KJV). The same urgency can be seen in the life of Jesus Christ who said, "We must work the works of Him who sent Me, as long as it is day; night is coming, when no man can work" (John 9:4).

THE TIME FACTOR

Any athlete knows the last minutes of a contest are the most crucial. How many games have been decided after the two-minute warning? As the game approaches a conclusion, strength is often spent. It would be easy for the athlete to yield, give up, and throw in the towel. But if he's looking to win, he hangs tough to the end. This is the time for his best shot.

Our culture emphasizes retirement, encouraging us to hang up the spikes and enjoy a fantasy fling. Even this is contrary to the game plan. In most cases when the two-minute warning sounds, the contest intensifies. For some, this is true of life as well. Ninety-four-year-old Simon of Cambridge illustrates this view as he said, "I cannot but run with all my might for I am close to the goal."[1]

The passion to be all that God wants us to be keeps us going no matter what. It means embracing an unbreakable spirit and adopting a positive attitude that will not accept defeat. It's knowing in our hearts that the prize is worth the price.

DON'T TURN BACK

We read in the Bible that the temptation the Hebrews faced was to return to their old way of life because they thought they would be free of adversity. But the writer of Hebrews consumes eleven chapters challenging his readers not to turn back. He challenges them to go on to maturity, to face head-on the responsibility to grow up in Jesus, to persevere in the faith.

Hebrews 11 is called the great "Hall of Faith" because it lists the godly individuals who made it to their goal. The question to readers is: *They made it. Why can't you?*

The writer exhorts his readers by adding, "Let us press on to maturity" (Heb. 6:1). Let us cease to contemplate the possibility of quitting and with perseverance finish the course that is set before us. He continues his call to steadfastness in Hebrews 12:1–2—a tough passage.

I'm reminded of something that happened several years ago when our daughter Becky was a patient at Parkland Hospital in Dallas. Pearl and I were on our way to visit her and were frustrated in our efforts to find a parking place. When I rounded a sharp corner and saw an empty space, I darted toward it, only to be greeted by a sign that simply said, "Don't even think about parking here!" We didn't.

The Hebrews writer is saying the same thing. Don't think of going back to your old ways, don't become stagnant in your faith now. He longs for readers to put it all together in one grand finale. He wants them to light up the night sky with fireworks celebrating a fabulous finish—to hang in there and do what must be done to reach the goal.

Running to win requires a winning attitude, a mind-set which focuses on finishing well. As Paul said, "We are taking every thought captive to the obedience of Christ" (2 Cor. 10:5).

THE MOTIVATION

Effective athletes in any field of competition begin with the end in mind. Before the contest, Olympic competitors visualize themselves receiving the gold medal. They think about the race, experience it, feel it, taste it. They stand in the empty stadium and hear enthusiastic fans cheering them on. In their thoughts they compete a thousand times before the race actually begins.

Did you know that as Christians we also receive applause from heaven's grandstands? That's why the writer of Hebrews urges his readers to have confidence and to persevere so we might receive the promises of God. He urges us to:

> Lay aside every impediment and every sin which hinders.
> Run the race set before us and keep moving forward.
> Fix our eyes upon Jesus, the source and goal of faith.

Many years ago I had the privilege of lacing up my running shoes and jogging a few miles in the Olympic stadium in Athens, Greece. Meditating on the Hebrews verses, I imagined being surrounded by the unseen believers in the stands. Those who themselves had finished well were now clapping for me. They believed I would cross the finish line victoriously, and I didn't want to disappoint them.

Charles E. Jones paints much the same picture in *Life Is Tremendous!*: "Wouldn't it be great if life were a game? Wouldn't it be wonderful if the field of life had cheering sections on each side, and when we reached the impossible situation and didn't know how to go on and no one understood us and we're about ready to fold and say those terrible words, 'I quit,' wouldn't it be wonderful if the stands would come alive and they'd yell, 'Charlie, boy, keep on going; we're with you!' I'd say, 'Whooooo! That's all I needed.' Boy, I'd go on down the field to another touchdown!"[2]

What does all this mean in practical terms? It means when problems arise in a marriage, we are committed to work them out. We identify our sins (pride, selfishness, insensitivity, whatever), confess them, and forsake them so they do not become a hindrance. Then we trust God as we look ahead. We are committed to keeping our marriage together because we made a promise to God that we would. We unleash His supernatural power to help us do it when we exercise our faith and keep moving according to His will.

When adversity comes, we can remember that God's plan is unfolding and it becomes an opportunity for us to be trained in righteousness. By seeking the Lord, we can find out what He wants us to learn through our difficult times.

While teaching a Bible conference in Saint John, New Brunswick, Pearl and I met a precious lady who epitomizes the type of saint who is running the race at full speed and will one day be sitting in the stands rooting for the next generation.

She recently wrote to thank me for one of my books, "It's just what I need to keep me on track as I live out my days, and endeavor to bring glory to God for all He has done for me all through my life of eighty-eight years." Mae inspires us as her focus is on the race and on the Savior. May her tribe increase.

Thus we find encouragement through the faithfulness of those who have gone before us and of those who live today. We're also motivated by the future—knowing that someone is watching how we respond to life's situations. Our faith paves the way for future generations to remain true.

Does this mean we will never have our low times? Not at all. In an interview with Dave Dravecky, Tim Stafford learned about one of Dave's most discouraging moments. He writes a conversation about Dave's first entering the major leagues on a trial basis. After a disappointing performance, Dave talks with his wife, Janice.

> "Well, David," she said sweetly, "why can't you throw strikes? What's wrong?"
>
> "Because when I get out there I'm clueless, Janice," I said. "When I get on the mound, I don't know where I'm throwing the ball. I don't know where the plate is. I start thinking that I'm in the big leagues, and these are big-league hitters, and I can't concentrate. I get the heebie-jeebies. I'm scared, Janice."
>
> For Janice it was an amazing and moving moment. She had never heard me admit to being scared. I had never opened up to her in weakness. We were talking about my feelings in a way we never had before. She began crying. She knew I couldn't cry for myself, so she cried for me.
>
> After holding each other and talking, Janice reminded me, "Remember? You and Byron used to say you should pitch as though Jesus Christ is your only audience."

> I felt better after I talked with Janice. Her words made me remember who I was and what really mattered.
>
> I got into that night's game in relief. When I reached the mound I took a deep breath, looked around, and thought of Jesus as my only audience. I couldn't fail, really.[3]
>
> That night Dave threw strikes and he was in the major leagues to stay, but he learned an important lesson about priorities. "Live life as though Jesus Christ were your only audience."[4]

While we may not be major-league pitchers, we can learn from Dravecky's experience. He realized that his job was to play his best for the glory of God, not for his own personal glory. In doing so, the pressure was off. He could relax because even if he lost a game, it wouldn't change the fact that God was still there. The same is true for us.

Our impetus to persevere lies not only in the past, present, and future, but also in our desire to play the game of life well for our Lord and Savior, Jesus Christ. What greater motivation could we need?

THE METHOD

We know why we keep running but how can we do it? Again, the admonitions in Hebrews 12:1–2 are the key.

The first exhortation is to lay aside every encumbrance or impediment. In other words, you can't win if you are weighted down. You can't win hanging on to hindrances.

A number of years ago I participated in a marathon in Houston, Texas, in January. It was quite cold in the early morning but as the day progressed, the weather became much warmer. Consequently, the course was actually littered with beautiful running suits, hats, gloves, and other garments worn to keep runners warm early, but unneeded in the later heat.

As Christians we sometimes hang on to hindrances that limit our effectiveness. Like those who seriously run for a prize and fling away the extraneous garments, we need to discard the old thought patterns and habits and put on the new.

F. B. Meyer writes, "Thousands of Christians are like water-logged vessels. They cannot sink; but they are so saturated with inconsistencies, and worldliness, and permitted evil, that they can only be towed with difficulty into the celestial port."[5]

In order to become Christlike, we lay aside our old self so that we can be renewed by the Holy Spirit working within. The apostle Paul advises us to "lay aside the deeds of darkness and put on the armor of light" (Rom. 13:12).

In laying aside impediments and hindrances, we examine ourselves honestly before God. The following scriptures admonish us to do this:

> But let a man examine himself. (1 Cor. 11:28)
> Test me, O LORD, and try me, examine my heart and my mind; for your love is ever before me, and I walk continually in your truth. (Ps. 26:2–3 NIV)
> Having therefore these promises, dearly beloved, let us cleanse ourselves from all filthiness of the flesh and spirit, perfecting holiness in the fear of God. (2 Cor. 7:1 KJV)
> Create in me a pure heart, O God, and renew a steadfast spirit within me. (Ps. 51:10 NIV)
> Beloved, I urge you as aliens and strangers to abstain from fleshly lusts, which wage war against the soul. (1 Pet. 2:11)

We are also to lay aside the sin of unbelief. The writer of

Hebrews challenges us to continue in the faith and not to depart from it.

A practical way to deal with sin is to apply 1 John 1:9 which says, "If we confess our sins, he is faithful and just to forgive us our sins, and to cleanse us from all unrighteousness" (KJV).

When we become aware of sin, we:

Confess it to the Heavenly Father immediately
Agree with Him that it needs to go
Ask for His grace in overcoming it.

The more we apply these three steps promptly in regard to a specific sin, the greater progress we will make in overcoming it.

A few years ago I used a surgeon's glove as a visual aid when giving a talk to young people. Holding up the glove, I pointed out that in order for the surgeon to use it, four things must be true. The glove had to be:

1. Clean
2. Empty
3. Available
4. Filled with the surgeon's hand

So it is with us if we are to be used by God in the process of daily living. To be a useful vessel for God, we are:

Cleansed through confession
Filled with the Holy Spirit
Strengthened by the Lord Jesus Christ.

Pearl and I attended Northwestern College in Minneapolis, Minnesota. (I will be eternally grateful for those years because it was there I met my sweetheart.) During one of the chapel services we can still remember the response to a simple message from the Word. Students began confessing sin and asking forgiveness. The captain of the basketball team admitted that he was not a believer. Students were on their knees all over the auditorium. Huddled in small groups, students were seeking God's face. This went on for a couple of days as our school tasted the sweet fruit of revival. The presence of the Spirit was very evident and God was at work. I find myself often praying, "O God! Do it again! Do it again!"

In his book, *Men Who Win,* Pastor Steve Lawson writes of Hebrews 12:1: "The Greek word for race (*agon*) is the very word from which we get the English word *agony.* Literally, Hebrews 12:1 says, 'Let us run with endurance the agony set before us.' Did you hear that? Agonizing. A blessed agony, yes. But agony, nevertheless—grueling, demanding, draining, stressful, taxing, tiring, torturing. Don't let anyone tell you otherwise."[6]

In my earlier days when someone would ask how many miles I had run that day, I'd always say five, eight, ten, fifteen, or something like that. But now even the tenths of a mile count. So I ran 3.6 miles this morning.

When I got to the 2.5 mark my mind started to say, "Quit. Why don't you just walk the rest of the way?" At that point something else kicked in—what I had learned in all those years of marathoning. There comes a time when you say no to the pain for the greater gain and you keep on running. When I got to the 3.6 marker my mind was saying, "Let's go for four!" But my body answered, "Go ahead, but if you do, I'm staying here."

As Christians we begin the race when we receive Jesus Christ as Savior and are born again into His family. We draw closer to Him as we run our race, and we cross the finish line when we are called into His presence. Sometimes we get weary and don't feel like running. However, it's perseverance through the tough times on earth that will strengthen our spiritual muscles and keep us moving toward our heavenly goal.

THE MODEL

While running the race, our eyes are not focused on another person, a ministry, a building, or an organization. Our eyes are fixed on Jesus Christ alone. We are beholding Him and He is molding us. He is our model.

The writer of Hebrews wrote, "fixing our eyes on Jesus, the author and perfecter of faith, who for the joy set before Him endured the cross, despising the shame, and has sat down at the right hand of the throne of God" (Heb. 12:1–2).

In examining this verse more closely, we see that having faith in the Lord Jesus means we have established a personal relationship with Him. And the goal of that relationship is expressed in another passage—"We shall be like Him, because we shall see Him just as He is" (1 John 3:2).

He is our source of faith because He came and gave His life. He is also faith's goal in that when we die here, we shall be with Him in Heaven.

He is also our model of perseverance because He endured the cross for the "joy set before Him." What is this joy? It's the anticipation of what lies ahead. The cross is something Jesus humanly would have liked to avoid: "My Father, if it is possible, let this cup pass from Me; yet not as I will, but as Thou wilt" (Matt. 26:39). Even though Jesus expressed the agony of the anticipated pain, He chose to bear the cross and poured out His life as a sacrifice for sin upon it.

The joy He experienced is a result of His obedience. He could have come down from the cross, but He chose to stay and fulfill His Father's plan. Consequently, Jesus has many brothers and sisters in the kingdom, and we are privileged to be part of it.

So many times in our Bible classes students have come up after the class and said, "You know, I almost didn't come tonight. I had all kinds of excuses but I came anyway. Look what I would have missed if I hadn't come. The Lord knew I needed this study; it was designed just for me!" That's the joy which is the fruit of obedience.

Jesus was also "despising the shame." Being made an open spectacle before mankind is not easy. Jesus despised the shame of dying in the public eye, but He continued on to victory, "and has sat down at the right hand of the throne of God." He completed His sacrificial work. The Lord never stopped running until He could sit down. He finished the course.

Military men are distinguished by their physical fitness, their ability to react quickly, and their stamina to overcome various obstacles. Out of the ranks of the military emerged many men who kept going until they literally sacrificed their lives for their country. Why does the soldier fight? Why does the athlete compete? To win! To do whatever is necessary in a given situation to achieve victory!

Listen to the Savior: "See, I stand knocking at the door. If anyone listens to my voice and opens the door, I will go into his house and dine with him, and he with me. As for the victorious, I will give him the honor of sitting beside me on my throne, just as I myself have won the victory and have taken my seat beside my Father on his throne. Let the listener hear what the Spirit says to the Churches" (Rev. 3:20–22 PHILLIPS).

CHAPTER NINE

Becoming Accountable

Keep thy heart with all diligence; for out of it are the issues of life.

PROVERBS 4:23 KJV

Once a party of six began a dangerous descent of a peak in the Swiss Alps. The first man in line lost his foothold and slipped over an icy ledge. The next two men slid after him, while the experienced climbers above braced themselves and stood firm to bear the shock.

When the rope ran its length, the cord snapped in two. The climbers watched in horror as their friends scrambled hopelessly to stop their slide over the slick precipice. Within seconds the men fell screaming to their deaths on the great glacier four thousand feet below.

For a half hour, the three remaining climbers were frozen in silence, terrified, unable to move. Finally, they resumed a slow, painstaking descent. Hours later they arrived safely in Zermatt, eager to find answers. Why had the rope broken? The survivors were shocked when a closer examination revealed the rope was a poor, and in this case, fatal substitute. True Alpine Club quality rope has a red strand running through it, but this rope did not.[1]

Mountain climbing requires athletic skill. Because climbing is done in group expeditions with participants roped together, the dexterity and expertise of each individual influences the outcome of the climb. If one climber slips on the rugged terrain, the other climbers will absorb the shock and, hopefully, save his life. The equipment is also critical.

Fortunately, the rope doesn't always break. Out there somewhere is a girl camper who was attached to our daughter, Julea's, rappelling rope in a camp training program some years ago. When the girl lost her footing, Julea stood her ground above, although the rope nearly pulled her in two until the camper could regain her footing.

Our son, Bobby, tells the story of when he and three buddies were roped together crossing a large snowfield. One of them unexpectedly fell, and it was such a surprise that the remaining three tripped also. The four boys slid almost four hundred feet down the snowfield until they were able to come to a stop just before reaching the rocks. Bobby laughs now when he recalls the incident and says, "Our only injuries were from our smoking jeans sliding at high speed across the snow!"

What do these stories illustrate? When we receive Christ we are born into a big family—God's family—with some on earth and some in heaven. Someday He'll call His family together. I can't wait!

Just as mountain climbers require partners, we need family members to nurture and stimulate our spiritual growth. They become a safeguard for treasures of the human spirit. "As iron sharpens iron, so one man sharpens another" (Prov. 27:17 NIV). "A friend loves at all times, and a brother is born for adversity" (Prov. 17:17 NIV). To disregard our need for a safety line and try the climb alone is dangerous.

Peter warns that Satan "prowls about like a roaring lion, seeking someone to devour" (1 Pet. 5:8), and he targets the wounded and stragglers in isolation from the herd. "Without good direction, people lose their way; the more wise counsel you follow, the better your chances" (Prov. 11:14 THE MESSAGE). When we learn to stay with the flock and lean on the Lord, God provides brothers and sisters to hold us accountable and to keep us on track.

This becomes a reality when we gather with other believers in a good church to study the Word and worship the Lord. What is your need at this time in your spiritual walk? Ask the Lord to lead you to the right person or persons who can help. Hook up, look up, and wake up to the joys of making progress in your walk with the Lord.

My only regret is that I didn't do this earlier in my Christian life. I would have been protected from many mistakes and blind spots. Since discovering the rich benefits of accountability, I've probably gone overboard, mainly because I see the wisdom in God's divine plan.

The rewards I'm reaping from these relationships are fourfold. I am a better:

Person: Everything in my life is scrutinized closely by others.
Partner: We have no secrets in our marriage.
Parent: I am more involved in the lives of my children and grandchildren.
Participant: I enjoy active involvement in the Lord's work.

In making our climb to maturity in Christ we, with our brothers and sisters, are all roped together by the Word of God. Our rope is genuine. God's truth has a scarlet thread (redemption of man through the blood of Christ) running from Genesis to Revelation. No substitute or counterfeit. It's the real thing. "I trust in your word" (Ps. 119:42 NIV).

SUBMISSION VS. INDEPENDENCE

To whom are we accountable? Our foremost accountability is to our Heavenly Father. This is **vertical accountability.** "For this reason, I bow my knees before the Father, from whom every family in heaven and on earth derives its name," (Eph. 3:14–15).

These verses remind us that God is sovereign. Therefore, because He is our Father, we submit to His authority, display our loyalty to Him, and bring honor to His name.

The Lord Jesus Christ is the head of the church—both the body of believers as a whole and each individual believer. Submission to the Lordship of Christ is a matter of the heart. I love to think of myself as being in His intensive care unit, wired to Him so He monitors my every move. "His eyes are on the ways of men; he sees their every step" (Job 34:21 NIV).

We are also accountable to our brothers and sisters in God's family. This is **horizontal accountability.** Our adversary is sharp. He knows exactly how to trip us up. When we're least expecting it, we may be overcome with fear, worry, discouragement, anger, bitterness, or impure thoughts. Then we need someone to come alongside us, someone we can talk to and pray with when we're under attack. Or we may be the one who must reach out to help another.

But how? God knows our frame—that we are weak and without wisdom to walk in His ways. That's why He has made provision through Christ. "For He delivered us from the domain of darkness, and transferred us to the kingdom of His beloved Son, in whom we have redemption, the forgiveness of sins" (Col. 1:13–14). "So that we confidently say, 'The Lord is my helper, I will not be afraid. What shall man do to me?'" (Heb. 13:6).

In the battle that Satan wages against God and His people, believers have a common interest. "For by one Spirit we were all baptized into one body, whether Jews or Greeks, whether slaves or free, and we were all made to drink of one Spirit" (1 Cor. 12:13). So when we make a decision to follow the Lord, it is to our advantage to let the Shepherd lead. He knows the way and all we have to do is follow.

The Scriptures clearly spell out our responsibilities to our brothers and sisters in the Church, the body of Christ. Verses with straightforward teaching about oneness, fellowship, commitment, motivation, sharing, comforting, loving, and forgiving are directed to the body of believers.

These Scriptures confirm that a church relationship is God's way of providing for our spiritual protection. So when we come together with other believers to pray, study God's Word, and encourage one another, we are obeying and submitting to God's plan and program. But when we disregard these resources and fail to function biblically in our relationships, we leave ourselves wide open for a shot from the pit.

The independent spirit began in the Garden of Eden when Adam chose to disobey God and do his own thing. His assertion of independence from God caused him and the entire human race a great deal of suffering. Before being saved we are slaves to sin in our lives. If we insist on going it alone, we are opening the door to certain defeat. We, too, are disobeying the Lord.

Ideally, our church is a way of bolstering our faith and helping us grow stronger in spiritual maturity. It is the equipping station for ministry. Its message is centered upon the Scriptures with its members being "doers of the word and not merely hearers..." (James 1:22).

WHAT IS A CHURCH?

Those who are called out make up His church—His bride—His body of which He is the Head. The **church invisible** is in heaven made up of believers who in physical death have gone home to be with the Lord.

The **church visible** is made up of those here on earth who have come to faith in the Lord Jesus Christ. It is universal in scope, (not confined to a certain denomination, type of building, or location), and rooted in the written Word and the Living Word, Christ Jesus.

Is it possible that some churches have fallen away from truth and biblical roots? Yes! That's why some practical criteria for establishing a church home are necessary. Seek a church that:

- Worships the one true and holy triune God—God the Father, God the Son, and God the Holy Spirit.
- Focuses upon Jesus Christ, the Son of God, our Savior, and soon coming King.
- Preaches and teaches the fully inspired, inerrant divine revelation, the Word of God.
- Administers the ordinances of baptism and the Lord's Supper.
- Exercises loving discipline and accountability.
- Encourages spiritual growth through Bible study groups, prayer, intimacy with Christ, works of ministry, and public witness to God's truth.
- Fosters fellowship, giving, and sacrificial concern for the lost and love for one another.

The word for fellowship in the New Testament Greek is *koinonia.* In his book *The Body,* Charles Colson describes this unique phenomenon. "Literally it *(koinonia)* means a communion, a participation of people together in God's grace. It describes a new community in which individuals willingly covenant to share in common, to be in submission to each other, to support one another and 'bear one another's burdens,' as Paul wrote to the

Galatians, and to build each other up in relationship with the Lord."[2]

As Christians we are called to be different than the sinful, selfish society in which we live. People can be unreasonable, illogical, and self-centered. I say—love them anyway. The more we love and serve others, the more we reflect Jesus to an unbelieving world. That is the mission of the church.

Paula D'Arcy in *Where the Wind Begins* writes, "We are called to reflect the light of love and to be that light in a mocking world. And we are all of us accountable to that love. Love is hard. It is threatening to think that our lives might be jarred, our money requested, our time demanded, our compassion tested, and our love exposed for what it really is, and for how far it really goes."[3]

John Mohr wrote a verse whose words speak of the necessity of making our lives a "sacrament of the present moment."

> Oh may all who come behind us find us faithful
> May the fires of our devotion light the way
> May the footprints that we leave
> Lead them to believe
> And the lives we lead inspire them to obey.[4]

BAPTISM

For the believer, baptism is symbolic of the decision he has made to follow Christ. Although Christians hold divergent views about the type of baptism, Scripture emphasizes its importance. Symbolically it pictures either the coming of the Spirit in the new birth by sprinkling or identification with the Savior's death, burial, and resurrection by immersion.

Jesus told the disciples, "All authority has been given to Me in heaven and on earth. Go therefore, and make disciples of all the nations, baptizing them in the name of the Father and the Son and the Holy Spirit, teaching them to observe all that I commanded you; and lo, I am with you always, even to the end of the age" (Matt. 28:18–20).

Baptism is a symbol of the power of the resurrected Christ within us and a reminder that we are walking in new life. After his baptism, Jesus was tempted by Satan. When our temptations come, we, like Jesus, can be victorious as we live in dependence upon our living Savior.

Over the years, administering the ordinance of baptism has brought me pure delight. The joy of the moment and the reality of the Lord's presence makes every celebration a special occasion.

THE LORD'S SUPPER

In addition to the ordinance of baptism, the Lord's Supper is another physical gesture reminding us of our oneness with Christ. Jesus Himself introduced this remembrance as a part of the Passover meal with His disciples in the upper room. The event is recorded in Scripture as follows: "And while they were eating, Jesus took some bread, and after a blessing, He broke it and gave it to the disciples, and said, 'Take, eat; this is My body.' And He took a cup and gave thanks, and gave it to them, saying, 'Drink from it, all of you; for this is My blood of the covenant, which is to be shed on behalf of many for forgiveness of sins.' But I say to you, I will not drink of this fruit of the vine from now on until that day when I drink it new with you in My Father's kingdom" (Matt. 26:26–29).

The significance of the Lord's Supper is highlighted by understanding the deliverance of Israel from Egypt's bondage. Each year, at the appointed time, Jewish families observed Passover which included: Killing a lamb without spot or blemish and preparing it for the family feast. **Symbol:** A picture of Christ's death.

At the first Passover, the blood of the lamb was to be placed in a basin, dipped with a bunch of hyssop (a mint-like plant), and sprinkled on the doorposts of the house. **Symbol:** We apply the promises of God to ourselves through faith—the hyssop. Our open profession of faith and obedience to Him is portrayed by the sprinkling of blood on the doorposts.

The feast of unleavened bread followed for seven days. **Symbol:** When following Christ we leave the old sin-filled life to walk in new truth.

All of this was in preparation for God's deliverance of the Israelites from bondage in Egypt. The Lord said, "On that same night I will pass through Egypt and strike down every firstborn—both men and animals—and I will bring judgment on all the gods of Egypt. I am the LORD. The blood will be a sign for you on the houses where you are; and when I see the blood, I will pass over you. No destructive plague will touch you when I strike Egypt" (Ex. 12:12–13 NIV).

The disciples knew the implication of the blood sacrifice. So Jesus began teaching the significance of the Lord's Supper by beginning with a familiar reference they understood, the Jewish Passover.

The Bread

Jesus once said, "I am the bread of life" (John 6:35). As He took the bread at the table, it portrayed nourishment for the spiritual man. Just as our physical bodies are nourished by bread, the spirits of believers are sanctified and sustained by the presence of Christ within us.

When Jesus broke the bread, the symbolic picture depicted Christ's broken body that would be hammered to a Roman cross the next morning. "He was crushed for our iniquities" (Isa. 53:5). When Jesus gave the bread to the disciples, he told them to "Take, eat; this is My body" (Matt. 26:26). "This is My body which is given for you; do this in remembrance of Me" (Luke 22:19).

Paul refers to the feast of unleavened bread during the Passover: "Clear out every bit of the old yeast that you may be new unleavened bread! We Christians have had a Passover Lamb sacrificed for us—none other than Christ himself! So let us keep the feast with no trace of the yeast of the old life, nor the yeast of vice and wickedness, but with the unleavened bread of unadulterated truth!" (1 Cor. 5:7–8 PHILLIPS).

Leaven or yeast in Scripture refers to sin. We are unfit to stand before God apart from Christ's forgiveness. This is why Paul warns the Christians in Corinth: "Therefore whoever eats the bread or drinks the cup of the Lord in an unworthy manner, shall be guilty of the body and the blood of the Lord. But let a man examine himself, and so let him eat of the bread and drink of the cup" (1 Cor. 11:27–28).

The Cup

Just as Jesus referred to His body in sacramental language, He also refers to His blood as represented by wine or grape juice. Before the momentous occasion of Jesus and His disciples partaking of the Lord's Supper together, animals provided sacrificial blood offered by the priests to God.

In the Old Testament Abraham and Isaac went up the mount of sacrifice and God provided a ram for a sacrifice thus sparing Isaac. Not this time! God the Father sees justice satisfied in the sacrifice of His sinless, spotless Son who is the Lamb who takes away the sin of the world. His blood is shed for many, not just a few. The reconciliation between God and man is offered to all who will receive Him.

During the Passover, Jesus is telling His disciples, "I am the sacrifice." Today, in remembrance of His death, we drink grape juice in a similar ceremony. Jesus tells the disciples He will soon be leaving, and that He will not be sharing the Lord's Supper with them again until they share it in His kingdom.

The passage ends as they sing a hymn and go for a quiet walk in the moonlight along the Kidron Valley. Each man seems to be alone in his thoughts, trying to figure everything out. The day of eternal redemption was about to dawn.

ACCOUNTABILITY

The thirteen men have been roped together in a relationship that has lasted for three years. Tonight they have already had one casualty and the other eleven belong on injured reserve, the walking wounded. All of this is on the eve of the biggest battle in eternity for the hearts of men.

Peter, the CEO of the operation, makes his public statement of loyalty: "Even though all may fall away, yet I will not" (Mark 14:29).

Jesus responds by saying: "Truly I say to you, that you yourself this very night, before the cock crows twice, shall three times deny Me" (Mark 14:30).

Peter doesn't take that sitting down. He fires off another volley: "'Even if I have to die with You, I will not deny You!' And they all were saying the same thing, too." (Mark 14:31). Talk is cheap! Put your money where your mouth is! Come on, guys, step up to the plate!

The facts are:

The executive committee of Peter, James, and John slept through the preparatory prayer meeting.

When Judas and his henchmen came: "They all left Him and fled" (Mark 14:50).

They cut the rope of responsibility and ran, leaving behind a pile of unfulfilled obligations.

It's easy for us to criticize the disciples but perhaps we should evaluate ourselves. How many relationships do we have that go beyond the surface? Relationships with people who know everything about us and yet remain committed to us? They'll be there to die in the trenches with us if necessary. They won't bother to check their Daytimer to see if they can make it to our funeral. They'll be there!

Just as Jesus had twelve, each of us needs a few relationships to keep us faithful, fruitful, and capable of making a strong finish. Our spiritual brothers and sisters are available for this very purpose. We need to be accountable, responsible, and functioning in Christ's body. For each one of us, the goal is to grow in righteousness, to draw closer to the Savior.

Meeting regularly with a small group forces us to deal with the real issues in our lives which hinder us from being an effective witness for Christ. The agenda for such a meeting might include: Bible study, Scripture memory, reading a good book chapter by chapter, prayer, and sharing. Living in openness and transparency will bear the rich fruit of joy and peace.

In short, we need each other. Just as mountain climbers band together to tackle their challenge, so we cannot make it alone in the Christian life. Thus we encourage one another day after day.

Christmas of 1995 has a special memory for me. Pearl called the office early Saturday morning, December 23, asking me if I could make three stops on the way home to pick up some things she needed for our Christmas celebration. That afternoon I drove to the crowded shopping center and parked strategically between my three stops. I made the first two stops in record time. Gloating about my good fortune, I was racing toward the final stop when it happened.

My tennis shoe struck a curb that I missed seeing through my bifocals, and I bit the concrete. Stunned by the blow to my head

I raised up to survey the damage. My glasses were badly bent but unbroken. The plastic bags were ripped with their contents scattered on the sidewalk, and my hand and arm were bleeding from lacerations. A lady rushed to my side and asked, "Are you hurt?"

My pride made me say, "No! I am OK!" I fumbled to gather my belongings in the gaping bags and, as I started to rise, I dispersed the contents once again all over the concrete. I'll always remember what happened next.

A little boy stepped out of the crowd of onlookers, handed me a large empty paper sack, and then turned and walked away. Evidently, he observed my predicament and had emptied his sack of treasures so he could meet my need.

At times, each of us feels like our lives are splattered all over the sidewalk, but we may be afraid to ask for assistance. My challenge for you is, first, ask God to make you sensitive, so you can reach out and touch someone today. Secondly, with a spirit of brokenness ask God to make you humble enough to receive the help of those who really care about you! Even if it's a little child.

CHAPTER TEN

Running Victory Laps

It is to God alone that we have to answer for our actions.

ROMANS 14:12 PHILLIPS

As international athletes prepared for the summer games, others transported the Olympic torch to Atlanta, Georgia. We usually think of victory laps *following* an event, but on May 20, 1996, an athlete who carried the Olympic flame celebrated his victory *before* the games officially began.

Tony Wakefield of Greenville, Texas, paralyzed by a 1975 high school football injury, was chosen to move the torch through Dallas via his motorized wheelchair. When everything was ready he warned bystanders, "Watch out! I'm putting this thing in high gear." Then he roared off into the heart of downtown Dallas, through the historic Dealy Plaza and toward the station where he would light the next bearer's torch.

Spirited supporters lined the route as Tony successfully maneuvered through the streets. His escorts could barely run fast enough to keep up. Friends, family, and children from the middle school where Tony works, squealed, cheered, and waved encouraging banners. In response, the quadriplegic's smile matched the rays of sunshine bouncing off the high-rise buildings.

When he stopped, Tony was the center of attention for a throng of reporters and news media. His mother, JoAnne, kissed Tony's cheek while his sponsor, Charles Davidson, squeezed his hand. Tony had successfully completed his part in the human chain linking Americans with the Olympic games.

To those who know Tony, he is a winner. His enthusiastic participation in the Olympic torch relay is just another demonstration of his courage and determination. Tony is a Christian gentleman with a heart for God and a genuine concern for others. Victory doesn't get any sweeter than it was for Tony and his community that day.[1]

Tony's example reminds us that triumph is not always related to physical ability, but is often linked to our attitude about life and how we live it. As a teenager whose future drastically changed in a moment of time, he did not become bitter. Rather, he has become an inspiration. Tony's rewards in heaven will far exceed the value of any olympic gold medal he might have won on earth.

What about eternal rewards? Is it wrong to seek them? Christians often ask these questions. They ask about life after death. What happens when I die? Will I really have to give an account?

Paul, writing to the Corinthians shares, "We are of good courage, I say, and prefer rather to be absent from the body and to be at home with the Lord. Therefore also we have as our ambition, whether at home or absent, to be pleasing to Him. For we must all appear before the judgment seat of Christ, that each one may be recompensed for his deeds in the body, according to what he has done, whether good or bad" (2 Cor. 5:8–10).

Professor Howard Hendricks loves to tell the story of the slalom skier who skied the downhill in world-record time. He burned the course, only to find he was disqualified. Complaining to the judge about the call, he heard the words: "You missed the flags!" The disgruntled competitor was heard saying: "What flags?"

Paul lived his life with this possibility: "But I bruise my body and make it my slave, lest possibly, after I have preached to others, I myself should be disqualified" (1 Cor. 9:27).

As believers we want to understand God's plan for rewards. We like to talk about the love of God but shrink from the idea of the Father being a judge. In his book, *Knowing God*, J. I. Packer shares four thoughts related to God as judge:

> **The judge is a person with authority.** Since God is our owner and maker, He writes the rules. He has a right to make moral laws for us and to reward us according to whether or not we keep them.
> **The judge is a person identified with what is good and right.** God loves righteousness and hates iniquity. Any judge who has no interest in seeing right triumph over wrong has an unbiblical view. God does not leave us in doubt about where he stands on life's issues.
> **The judge is a person of wisdom to discern truth.** We may fool men, but we cannot fool God. He is omniscient. He knows us and judges us as we really are. He judges according to factual truth as well as moral truth.
> **The judge is a person of power to execute sentence.** Modern judges only pronounce the sentence, another official carries it out. But God does it all.[2]

Does this make us fear God?

THE FEAR OF THE LORD

When we talk about the fear of the Lord, I like to remember the three Rs:

Respect for God—Recognize His authority and know I am accountable to Him.

Responsibility to God—I am responsible to God because I am His child.

Relationship—Since I am related to Him people will see me and think of Him.

Paul explains that as believers we will give an account at the judgment seat of Christ. This is not to be confused with the GWT judgment—great white throne judgment—for unbelievers. "And I saw a great white throne and Him who sat upon it, from whose presence earth and heaven fled away, and no place was found for them. And if anyone's name was not found written in the book of life, he was thrown into the lake of fire" (Rev. 20:11–15). For those who have not received Christ as Savior are thrown into the lake of fire. Nobody survives.

But the believer will have a different kind of judgment. You might think of it like this. We live in a temporary tent. When we die we'll go to our permanent home where we'll meet Christ face to face. All believers will be accountable for their stewardship of time, talents, and treasures while on earth.

THE JUDGMENT SEAT OF CHRIST

It's a sure thing. No one will be exempt. Sometimes I receive a jury summons, but many times I'm out of town and unable to serve. So I'm pardoned from jury duty. But at the judgment seat of Christ, we must all appear—no excuses, no exceptions.

I like to think of it like this. At the moment of our new birth, a computer printout begins on our lives which will be audited at the judgment seat of Christ. When will the audit happen? In my personal opinion, it will occur in heaven during the seven years of tribulation on earth.

I believe the next prophetic event will be the Rapture of the Church (more about this later). Following the Rapture, the drama of the tribulation begins on earth with worldwide government and terrible events we can't even imagine. But after believers are removed from the earth, I believe we will go before the judgment seat of Christ.

Why? To receive rewards for faithfulness while on earth. Dr. Joe Wall, author of the book *Going for the Gold,* discusses the importance of understanding future rewards. He says, "My interest in the judgment seat of Christ goes back to my early days as a Christian. After becoming a Christian as a young teenager, I attended a Bible study taught by a man devoted to in-depth doctrinal teaching. Under his instruction I first heard what the Bible had to say about the judgment seat of Christ and began to understand that every thought, every word, every deed, and every motive will one day be evaluated by Jesus. So while still in high school, I began making life decisions based on an awareness that someday I would have to give account of my life to Jesus."[3]

Understanding the judgment seat and being aware that Christ could return at any moment should inspire us to godly living. "And everyone who has this hope fixed on Him purifies himself, just as He is pure" (1 John 3:3). Such knowledge will cause us to become more alert to the eternal importance of our thoughts, words, and actions—and will also increase our anticipation of His appearing, called the Rapture.

THE RAPTURE

A bumper sticker reads: "In case of Rapture this car will be unmanned." Barbara Johnson, author and speaker, signs off with: "He's going to toot and I am going to scoot." Pearl and I have two flight-attendant friends who are training their dogs to jump high. They call it rapture practice! I have questioned their theology but all to no avail.

The Rapture of the Church is the next prophetic event on God's calendar. It could happen any day! The exciting thing about all this is that we are one day closer than we were yesterday.

Scripture teaches about this. Some facts are found in 1 Thessalonians 4:13–18 (paraphrased):

> The Lord Himself (in His glorified body) will descend from heaven with a shout.
> The voice of the archangel will be heard along with the trumpet of God.
> The believers who have already died shall rise up from their graves first with new incorruptible bodies.
> Then believers who are still living on earth will instantly be changed and ushered into the Lord's presence, bypassing the gateway of physical death.
> Both groups will be caught up in the clouds to meet the Lord in the air.

Another verse which describes this event says, "Behold, I tell you a mystery; we shall not all sleep, but we shall all be changed, in a moment, in the twinkling of an eye, at the last trumpet; for the trumpet will sound, and the dead will be raised imperishable, and we shall be changed" (1 Cor. 15:51–52).

I once saw a sign on the door of a church nursery that described their babies in a similar way—"They shall not all sleep, but they shall all be changed." I find myself often singing that wonderful little chorus; "Soon and very soon, we are going to see the King…" One little boy really got excited when he thought he heard his mother singing: "Soon and very soon, we are going to Burger King…"

When will Christ come for His own? Paul, seemed eager to go to glory with his running shoes on. He says as much in Philippians 3:11, "In order that I may attain to the resurrection from the dead." Although the moment also known in Scripture as the Day of Christ never came for the apostle, it might well come for us. Who knows?

The glorious hymn, "It Is Well with My Soul" captures the excitement:

> "And Lord, haste the day when the faith shall be sight,
> The clouds be rolled back as a scroll,
> The trump shall resound and the Lord shall descend,
> Even so, it is well with my soul."[4]

Realizing the next instant could be our last here and our first with Him, causes us to stop and ponder a few questions. What am I doing with my time, my talents, my life? Perhaps the uncertainty will cause us to start living with a looser hand and a sharper focus.

Here's my paraphrase of what Jesus said to His men in the upper room only hours before the cross: "Stop being troubled in your heart; be putting your trust in God. Also, be putting your trust in Me. In the house of My Father there are many dwelling places. If it were not so, I would have told you; for I am going to prepare a place for you. And if I go and prepare a place for you, I will come again, and will receive you to Myself; in order that where I am, you may be also" (John 14:1–3).

People who have loved ones over on the other side find great comfort in knowing they will soon be reunited with their loved ones. Jim and Fran Sandin experienced the heartbreaking sorrow of losing their seventeen-month-old son, Jeffrey. In her book, *See You Later, Jeffrey,* Fran writes:

> One day while reflecting upon the rich lessons I'd learned since Jeffrey's departure, I remembered a note I'd written

soon after he left us. When I found it and read it over again, the words still brought comfort and hope.

Dear Jeffrey,

There was something very special about you from the beginning. I could not explain it. Perhaps it was the twinkle in your bright blue eyes or your zest for life. You were with us for such a short time, but Daddy and I loved you very much. We enjoyed every minute. Steve and Angie loved you, too. We all miss you and wish you were with us, but the Good Shepherd gathered you into His gentle arms and took you to a better place. As I walk with the Lord each day, I know I am close to you. We'll see you later, Jeffrey. Then, we'll be together forever.

I love you dearly,
Mom[5]

Since the beginning of time, death has caused separation. When we know Christ, our separation is only temporary. How good to know we will have a reunion in eternity!

REWARDS AT THE BEMA

Paul uses the word *bema* to describe the time when Jesus evaluates our lives. The *bema* judgment occurs following the Rapture, and it is not a relational issue. It is a matter of recognition and rewards. The primary focus is not sin but stewardship. The penalty for sin has been canceled forever at the cross. The *bema* is fruit-inspection time. What has the Spirit accomplished in us and through us?

The evaluation done within God's family is not for punishment but for rewards—for the faithfulness or unfaithfulness of the believer as a servant. Two kinds of servants are described in 1 Corinthians 3:10–15.

1. The spiritual believer: With Christ as the foundation of the building of salvation, the service of the spiritual believer (works done under the guidance and in the power of the Holy Spirit) will remain. When Jesus looks upon the believer with eyes like a flame of fire (Rev. 1:14), the works of the spiritual believer are like gold, silver, and precious stones. They will not be burned up by the judgment.

2. The carnal believer: The believer who does not allow the Holy Spirit to work through him but obeys the desires of his flesh has works described as wood, hay, and straw which will burn up under the scrutiny of Jesus. The believer will still be saved because his salvation is not at stake, but his works will be burned up. In other words, he escapes judgment with smoldering pants.

Scripture emphasizes that as believers our bodies are the temples of the Holy Spirit. Just as a physical temple of worship should not be desecrated, neither should our bodies. We are to avoid living by worldly wisdom and flee the sins of the flesh. By living a carnal life, we forfeit eternal rewards. After all, the prize is given to faithful servants who give glory, praise, and honor to the Lord. He has provided for our every need.

Paul's descriptions of rewards remind us of the Olympic games in his day. The competitors reported at daybreak and took an oath that they were of pure Hellenic (Greek) blood, had never committed a wrong, had trained faithfully, and would not resort to any underhandedness in competition.

"Contests included foot races, wrestling, boxing, the pentathlon, horse races, and chariot races. At the end of the Olympic festival, contestants appeared before the platform of the judgment, the *bema*. If the judge proclaimed that an individual had won and had not been disqualified for some reason, that competitor received a crown of olive branches.

"As the victor, he would normally return to his home city for a hero's welcome. The townspeople, seeking to distinguish him, often would erect a statue in his honor, give him choice seats at public events, and exempt him from taxes."[6]

In the passages where Paul discusses rewards, he compares the Christian life to a track meet and a boxing match, two major events in the games: "Do you not know that those who run in a race all run, but only one receives the prize? Run in such a way that you may win. And everyone who competes in the games exercises self-control in all things. They then do it to receive a perishable wreath, but we an imperishable. Therefore, I run in such a way, as not without aim; I box in such a way, as not beating the air; but I buffet my body and make it my slave, lest possibly, after I have preached to others, I myself should be disqualified (1 Cor. 9:24–27).

Paul is urging us to take our Christian life seriously, to avoid moral compromise because we, too, will stand before the judgment seat of Christ.

At the *bema* we will be rewarded for what God thinks is important. Whatever works we have done, as a result of the fruit of the spirit within, will be an outward indication of the reality of our walk with and love for God.

In summary, salvation is a free gift of God by His grace and cannot be earned. However, the rewards given at the *bema* are earned by a believer after he has received Christ. The person who tries in his own strength to produce good deeds has nothing of value to present to Jesus at the *bema*. But the one who is living in an abiding fellowship with Christ will have something to present of lasting value.

How can we prepare for the *bema*? Here are three ways. We can:

1. Guard our relationship with the Lord by maintaining fellowship.

2. Be faithful in our disciplines: Bible study, prayer, witnessing, giving.

3. Serve others with our spiritual gift or gifts: Teaching, Exhortation, Mercy…

In this way, our record of sins is cleared in advance of the *bema*. Through our confession, God erases the sin tapes.

Some Christians will be honored at the *bema*, but others will be ashamed. Why? Scripture gives a few possibilities.

Failure to persevere in faith (Mark 9:19)
Stagnant in their walk with God (Heb. 6:12)
Started eagerly in their Christian walk, but gave up when the going got tough (Heb. 12:1–17)
Unwilling to serve the Lord or indulging in selfishness (2 Pet. 2:10)
Grasping after earthly treasures (Matt. 6:19–20)
Squandering education, wealth, opportunity, or talent (Matt. 25:14–30)
Following false teachers (2 John 7–8)
Motivated by recognition of men (Matt. 6:1–18)

Also 1 John 2:28 seems to be telling us that one who is impure and indulges in that which is disgraceful for a child of God will experience great shame in Christ's presence.

Thus the doctrine of the judgment seat of Christ is a powerful motivation for godly living and should encourage us to:

- Set proper goals for our lives
- Recognize our need for good stewardship of our time, money, and talents

- Keep walking in faith, even when circumstances are difficult
- Confess our sins and aspire to live holy lives
- Work toward spiritual maturity and look forward to Christ's coming[7]

THE WREATH CROWNS

When modern-day Olympians win a contest, they are awarded a gold medal, indicating they are tops in their field of competition. But in New Testament days, a garland of woven branches of wild olive leaves, pine needles, laurel, or parsley was placed on the winner's head to signify victory. It was the same as getting the blue ribbon or the first-place trophy.

Two Greek words for crown are *stephanos* and *diadem*. In the New Testament, the *diadem* is reserved for royalty. Only Jesus Christ will wear the *diadem*.

The believers will wear another type of crown, the wreath-crown, the *stephanos*. Paul refers to this in 1 Corinthians 9:25—"And everyone who competes in the games exercises self-control in all things. They then do it to receive a perishable wreath, but we an imperishable."

When believers receive an award from Jesus, their crowns will not fall apart. They will last for eternity, and "We will cast these crowns before His throne."

To quote my favorite professor: "If that doesn't light your fire, you are using wet wood!"

Because we will stand face to face with Christ, we become acutely aware of our accountability. Are we living to please ourselves? Are our daily activities and choices honoring Him? This poem by an unknown author causes us to stop and think:

When I stand at the judgment seat of Christ
and He shows me His plan for me,
The plan of my life as it might have been, had He had
His way,
And I see how I blocked Him here and checked Him
there,
And I would not yield my will.
Will there be grief in my Saviour's eyes,
Grief though He loves me still?
He would have me rich,
But I stand there poor, stripped of all but His grace,
While memory runs like a hunted thing,
Down the paths that I can not retrace.
Then my desolate heart will well nigh break with the
tears I cannot shed.
I shall cover my face with my empty hands and bow
my uncrowned head.
Lord of the years that are left of me,
I give them to thy Hand.
Take me and break me,
Mold me to the pattern that Thou hast planned.[8]

Running the race is not always easy, convenient, or fun, but when we persevere, Christ rewards us. Perhaps we will someday identify with the 1996 Boston Marathon winner in this report:

> Uta Pippig kept falling farther and farther behind in Monday's 100th Boston Marathon. She almost dropped out after 4 miles, and even after 24 it seemed as if maybe she should have.

> But Pippig, a heavy favorite to capture a third straight title, overcame a 30 second deficit with 2.2 miles to go and won by 1 minute 25 seconds. "I felt not nice," the thirty-year-old German said: "I was thinking several times to drop out because it hurt so much. But in the end, I'm O.K. because I won."[9]

"Therefore also we have as our ambition, whether at home or absent, to be pleasing to Him. For we must all appear before the judgment seat of Christ that each one may be recompensed for his deeds in the body, according to what he has done, whether good or bad" (2 Cor. 5:9–10).

PART THREE

The Farmer

Chapter Eleven

Pulling Weeds

Be kind to each other; be understanding. Be as ready to forgive others as God for Christ's sake has forgiven you.

EPHESIANS 4:32 PHILLIPS

On a November Sunday night, James R. Upp Sr., M.D., a Louisiana pediatrician, answered a knock at his front door. The deputy sheriff began gently, "Diane's car veered off the road into a ditch. I'm sorry, Dr. Upp. She's dead."

Stunned, Dr. Upp stood speechless while the deputy continued, "We don't think it was an accident. We're treating it as a possible homicide."

Dr. Upp later learned that two seventeen-year-old boys on a drunken joyride had been throwing chunks of concrete at oncoming vehicles and a piece crashed through the windshield of his daughter's car. Vivacious Diane Simino, twenty-eight, married only one year, had devoted herself to working with teens. Now one pointless, senseless act snuffed out her life. How should Dr. Upp respond?[1]

When Alex and Dorothea got married each had a different definition of "a successful husband." He thought it was providing a good living for the family and she thought it meant pampering his wife and children.

When he landed a job with the Los Angeles Police Department, the problems escalated. The former policeman explains, "In a big city you're exposed to so very much—homicide, child molestation, accidents—you almost have to become cynical. I knew if I'd acknowledged my feelings, I couldn't have done my job. So when I got home, my feelings were buried."

Dorothea reacted with extreme disappointment. "I was raised to be overly dependent and felt it was up to Alex to make me happy; I didn't realize that happiness comes from within. When he was preoccupied with work, I handled it by getting more and more involved with our four children."

Alex and Dorothea Tingiride became two separate entities—no communication, short tempers, misunderstanding, financial pressures. Only one solution seemed viable. Divorce. But did a legal document end their pain?[2]

One day when an angry customer turned to leave, David Kiel thought the man was planning to return with some money that he owed. Instead, David heard a deafening explosion. He recounts, "When I awoke, I was on the floor. I couldn't move. Blood was streaming out of my mouth. Something was dreadfully wrong!"

"Twice I blacked out. When I came to, I was in a hospital in a canvas-strap apparatus called a Stryker Frame. From the nurses I pieced together what had happened. I had been shot in the back with a .38 caliber revolver. The bullet had hit just below the seventh cervical vertebra. Paramedics had probably saved my life, but doctors said I would never walk again. The injury to the spinal cord had caused permanent paralysis."[3]

How could David face this life-changing event?

FARMERS KNOW ABOUT WEEDS

Such hurtful, unpredictable, and upsetting occasions send us racing to punch the question key on the Father's hotline. Why me? Why this? Why now? What did I do to deserve this? With these issues left unresolved, we are tempted to become bitter.

Biblical characters were not exempt from similar responses. Naomi was no stranger to adversity. She lost her husband and two sons in Moab. When she returned to Bethlehem her first words were: "Don't call me Naomi," she told them. "Call me Mara, because the Almighty has made my life very bitter. I went away full, but the LORD has brought me back empty. Why call me Naomi? The LORD has afflicted me; the Almighty has brought misfortune upon me" (Ruth 1:20–21 NIV).

The author of the Book of Hebrews cautions his readers not to ignore the grace of God. Why? Because if we do, bitterness will take hold. Results? Many will be defiled. When we quit during difficult times we are essentially telling God that His grace ran out and we have a right to replace trust with bitterness.

Just as the Christian walk is compared to the soldier and the athlete, Paul includes the farmer in his analogy. Farmers are well-acquainted with weeds. If not controlled, weeds begin to dominate a crop. They can literally squeeze out healthy plants and reduce productivity. Likewise, when bitterness invades a human heart, the consequences are devastating to the one who is bitter and to others as well. But how can we avoid becoming bitter when such unjust and difficult circumstances invade our lives?

The simple answer is to avail ourselves of the resources of His grace. God never allows anything in our curriculum without providing adequate resources to triumph.

Most farmers use whatever method they can for weed control. Some use machinery called cultivators to break up the soil so weeds are uprooted. Land may be flooded with water to kill some types of weeds and drained to kill others. Weeds may be burned off the land or smothered by covering with hay or plastic sheets. Sometimes herbicides are necessary for weed control. However, God only uses one solution for the problem of bitterness which springs up in our hearts. Forgiveness. His grace is adequate for us to be able to forgive.

BITTERNESS OR FORGIVENESS?

Sometimes our problems are not as dramatic as the examples at the beginning of this chapter. They involve everyday difficulties in just getting along with one another.

Professional counselors label bitterness as the number one problem they encounter in treating the Christian community. Unresolved interpersonal conflicts are contributing factors. I am convinced the only surgery that will lance the boils of bitterness is forgiveness.

Still, we all agree that forgiveness is difficult. In his book *The Freedom of Forgiveness*, David Augsburger writes, "How do you forgive? Forgive when the cost is staggering, the pain unbearable, and your own just anger still swelling?"[4]

Author Lewis Smedes observes: "Forgiving seems almost unnatural. Our sense of fairness tells us people should pay for the wrong they do. But forgiving is love's power to break nature's rule."[5]

WHY IS FORGIVENESS SO DIFFICULT?

Even when we know we should forgive others, we often resist it. A biblical example of bitterness resulting in a family tragedy took place when Amnon, King David's firstborn, raped his half-sister, Tamar. Absalom, Tamar's full brother, waited two years for Daddy David to reprove Amnon. Although Absalom was furious, David did nothing. Absalom eventually took the law into his own hands and murdered Amnon. Then he fled to Geshur for three years. Once again David did nothing to mend his relationship with his estranged son, Absalom.

Finally General Joab interceded and convinced David to allow Absalom to return to Jerusalem. Although Absalom did return, fellowship was not restored. David said, "He must go to his own house; he must not see my face" (2 Sam. 14:24 NIV). For another two years Absalom lived in his own condominium in Jerusalem and never had an audience with his father. David made no effort to reconcile and forgive. After seven long years, the damage was done. It was too late. Once again Joab insisted that David take time to meet with his son.

David and Absolom had an emotional encounter, but nothing was really resolved. Their relationship was swept over the falls of neglect. Absalom tried to take the kingdom from his father by forming a well-orchestrated conspiracy but ended up a fatality on the field of battle. David was shaken, shattered, and sobbing, "O my son Absalom! My son, my son, Absalom! If only I had died instead of you—O Absalom, my son, my son!" (2 Sam. 18:33 NIV). The tragedy of the whole story is that David forgave an insignificant offense when a fellow named Shimei cursed and threw rocks at him, but he was unable to forgive his own son.

CONSEQUENCES OF BITTERNESS

A vicious cycle is often involved when people fail to forgive. Five steps are common.

1) First comes the *offense*, in this case Amnon's rape of Tamar.

2) Then *resentment* develops. Absalom resents his half-brother. He resents his father for not dealing with the offense.
3) Resentment grows to *hatred*. Absalom seethes at the injustice of it all.
4) Hatred, allowed to fester, becomes a lingering *grudge*. Absalom does not forget what happened.
5) Eventually the grudge begets a thirst for *revenge*. Absalom plots to kill. He throws a party at the ranch during sheep-shearing time and Amnon is history.

While the example of David and Absalom involves a father and son, marital heartbreak is often traced back to the five steps of this vicious cycle. Physical, verbal, sexual, and psychological abuse is normal fruit from weeds of bitterness. Partners becoming historical and hysterical at the same time set the stage for volatile confrontations.

DIFFERENT KINDS OF FORGIVENESS

Forgiveness can stop this cycle at any point. However, forgiveness is described in different ways.

Conditional forgiveness says, "I forgive you but don't do it again."
Partial forgiveness also implies, "I forgive you but don't expect me to forget what you have done to me." Or "Forgive your enemies but never forget their names."
Delayed forgiveness means, "I will forgive you, but give me some space to get over the hurt."
Immediate, unconditional forgiveness happens rarely indeed. Yet forgiveness is a prerequisite to genuine love. As Dan B. Allender writes, "I cannot hope to ever love

> someone unless I am committed to forgive him. I cannot hope to ever forgive him—that is, truly forgive him—unless I know the rich, incomprehensible joy of being forgiven."[6]

Forgiveness down here is related to fellowship up there. In other words it affects our prayer life. My understanding of 1 Peter 3:7 is Peter telling us husbands: "Husbands, in like manner, be living with your wives according to knowledge, showing honor unto the woman as the weaker vessel; as to those who are also joint heirs of the grace of life, in order that your prayers *may not be hindered.*"

Francis A. Schaeffer in his book, *The Mark of the Christian,* says, "Many Christians rarely or never seem to connect their own lack of reality and fellowship with God with their lack of forgiveness to men, even though they may say the Lord's Prayer in a formal way over and over in their weekly Sunday worship services. We must all continually acknowledge that we do not practice the forgiving heart as we should. And yet the prayer is, 'Forgive us our debts or our trespasses as we forgive our debtors or those who trespass against us.' We are to have a forgiving spirit even before the other person expresses regret for his wrong."[7]

Paul Adolph in his book, *Release from Tension,* points out: "The result of living in unforgiveness is like holding a tightly corked bottle under Niagara Falls while we wonder why never a drop of water enters it, despite the overabundance of water. The stopper must be removed in order that the bottle may be filled with water. Just so must the plug of selfish resentment be removed from us before we can enjoy the fullness of God's grace in forgiveness. May God help us to forget our resentments as He can forget. No more should we apologize for our poor memories when we forget some triviality."[8]

Staying on top of things and dealing with issues as they happen will keep us on the path to fellowship with God and good human relationships. I don't know about you, but I would dread the thought of ever living another day out of fellowship with my Heavenly Father.

CHECK THE INSTRUCTIONS

One of my all-time favorite Bible characters is Peter. He is a master at getting into deep yogurt and then calling Jesus to the rescue.

In Matthew 18 he had an altercation with somebody and he was wondering—how long must you do right to the one who is doing you wrong? I can just hear him asking in Matthew 18:21—"Lord, how often shall my brother sin against me and I shall forgive him? Up to seven times?"

You notice Peter doesn't make an issue over how many times he can *ask* for forgiveness. It's how far do I go in granting it before I drop the ax. Isn't it amazing that when we are seeking forgiveness we are begging for mercy and when we are granting it we are wanting justice?

Since the going rate was two, Peter multiplied that by three and added one for good measure fully expecting to hear his favorite commendation from the lips of our Lord: "Blessed are you, Simon Barjonas, because flesh and blood did not reveal this to you, but My Father who is in heaven" (Matt. 16:17).

Instead Peter is stunned when he hears Jesus respond, "I am not saying to you up to seven times, but up to seventy times seven." In Matthew 18:22 Jesus is saying, Quit keeping score! Cut the tapes, break the slate, burn the ledger. It is forgiveness without computation.

Paul speaks of pardon in Acts 24:16, "In view of this, I also do my best to maintain always a blameless conscience both before God and before men." The psalmist writes, "Great peace have they who love your law, and nothing can make them stumble" (Ps. 119:165 NIV).

In the New Testament, the word translated *forgiveness* has several meanings. My favorite is: "Let the pot drop." Don't you love it? Can't you see this person walking around carrying all of his resentments in this big pot and now he is instructed to drop it. Wow! what a relief. It can also mean: to leave, to let go, to send forth, to send away.

Hustling back to Matthew 18, it's story time. Jesus, having stated the principle of unlimited forgiveness, is now ready to give Peter a picture of what He means by using a parable. The cast of characters involves a king who is wanting to settle accounts with his servants. As the audit is proceeding, one of the CPAs brings the king a ledger that reveals a $12 million debt. This servant owes more than the total budget of the state in which he lives!

When the IRS lays hold of all his resources including his wife and children, they find he is far short of being able to clear his indebtedness. Terrified, the servant falls on his knees begging for time and promising to pay back all he owes.

The king is touched by this request and he releases him from custody and forgives his debt. The king's generosity is incredible! With a gift like that, the servant ought to be walking on cloud nine!

Instead of being grateful and generous, he finds a fellow servant who owes him twenty dollars and he makes a big deal out of it. He seizes him, squeezes him by the throat, and says: "Here's the IOU with your signature on it and I want you to give me that money now!"

The debtor says: "Please give me some time and I'll take care of this!" The servant will not hear of it, so he has him jailed until he figures out a way to pay his twenty-dollar debt. The king notices some of his law-enforcement people are pretty upset. After quizzing them, he is furious when he discovers what the servant has done. Consequently, the king withdraws his pardon and angrily hands over the servant to the prison authorities until his multimillion-dollar debt is retired.

The story's punch line is: "So shall My Heavenly Father also do to you, if each of you does not forgive his brother from your heart" (Matt. 18:35). We all have an impossible debt we owe to God, and He assumed the full responsibility for that debt by the death of His Son on the cross. We should be filled with gratitude and generosity as we view the insignificant debts of others toward us.

Paul tells the Ephesians: "And be kind to one another, tender-hearted, forgiving each other, just as God in Christ also has forgiven you" (Eph. 4:32). He instructs the Colossian saints: "Bearing with one another, and forgiving each other, whoever has a complaint against any one; just as the Lord forgave you, so also should you" (Col. 3:13). Forgiveness must become a way of life for us, if we ever expect our relationship with the Lord to grow.

Since Jesus has freed us from a phenomenal debt by forgiving our sins, shouldn't God's forgiveness move us to immediately reconcile with others? By forgiving, we free them and ourselves to live a new life filled with the love of the Spirit.

FOUR Rs OF UNFORGIVENESS

Unfortunately, we do not always respond with a forgiving heart, and our reluctance to obey hinders us from experiencing the blessings of God. The reasons are included in the four Rs.

Rights—We stand on them. I have my rights and he had no business doing that to me.
Resentment—I just can't stand him. He acts so smart.
Revenge—I am unwilling to forgive until revenge has been secured and just payment made for the wrong that

has been done. The revenge philosophy? Don't get mad—get even.

Reckoning—I have been keeping account of the wrongs done against me and I am now unwilling to forget. The ledger is too full.

BIBLICAL EXAMPLES OF FORGIVENESS

When we think we can't forgive, we can recall Joseph in the Old Testament. He wins a prize for some of life's toughest circumstances. It must have been excruciating for him to forgive. Ripped from his father's home when he was only a teenager and sold into slavery in Egypt, he could easily have hated the ten brothers who engineered his disappearance. If the same thing happened today, he could sue and win millions in damages for the physical abuse and emotional trauma he suffered.

Years later when he is tearfully reunited with his brothers, they tremble remembering what they did to their younger brother. But Joseph, recognizing the sovereignty of God in elevating him to a position of leadership, answers, "Don't be afraid. Am I in the place of God? You intended to harm me, but God intended it for good to accomplish what is now being done, the saving of many lives" (Gen. 50:19–20 NIV). Joseph responds further, promising to provide food for their families. He comforts and speaks kindly to them. Few illustrations of forgiveness are more touching.

In Paul's final letter he finds time for forgiveness and reconciliation with John Mark who had failed to follow through on an earlier missionary-journey commitment. Peter, in his final epistle, also demonstrates forgiveness and reconciliation with the apostle Paul.

But Jesus, hanging on the cross with spikes driven into His hands and feet, gives us the ultimate example of forgiveness when

He prays, "Father, forgive them; for they do not know what they are doing" (Luke 23:34).

YOU CAN DO IT

Unfortunately, we sometimes allow an offense to take root in our hearts which becomes a weed of bitterness. Like the farmer, if we fail to pull out or eradicate the weeds, they poison our whole being, hampering our relationship with God and with others. If we allow weeds to grow in our hearts, we will not be spiritually and emotionally healthy and whole. Honest forgiveness is the only antidote for bitter weeds.

Jesus shows the seriousness of the unforgiving heart in the Sermon on the Mount. In Matthew 5:23–24 He said, "If, therefore, you are presenting your offering at the altar, and there remember that your brother has something against you, leave your offering there before the altar, and go your way, first be reconciled to your brother, and then come and present your offering."

You want your worship to soar, but it will never leave the runway if you are trying to participate with an unforgiving heart. I am convinced that much of what the Lord would like to do in our lives never happens because we are unwilling to deal with our hostility and lack of forgiveness.

FOUR PRINCIPLES OF FORGIVENESS

Is it possible to forgive? Yes. Four principles will help us forgive those who have hurt us, even if we think it is impossible.

1. God is sovereign.

When we keep our eyes on our great God, His purposes and plans, we see people and relationships as part of something greater. Joseph's secret to personal victory in forgiving others was due to his focusing on God's bigger plan rather than on the disappointing people and circumstances around him. "You intended to harm me, but God intended it for good to accomplish what is now being done, the saving of many lives" (Gen. 50:20 NIV).

2. Skillful hands are molding and shaping us.

All of life's circumstances contribute to the ultimate goal of our becoming like Christ. As a recent book title suggests, life is a contact sport. Why do we become angry at the human equipment God uses to shape us? Some folks are put in our lives to be God's sandpaper to file and smooth our rough edges so we are of greater use to Him. If someone consistently makes us really angry, there's probably a greater reason.

3. The Spirit's power is present and available.

He is here, ready to walk us through the process of forgiving. "No temptation has overtaken you but such as is common to man; and God is faithful, who will not allow you to be tempted beyond what you are able, but with the temptation will provide the way of escape also, that you may be able to endure it" (1 Cor. 10:13). We are not alone. "And He has said to me, 'My grace is sufficient for you, for power is perfected in weakness.' Most gladly, therefore, I will rather boast about my weaknesses, that the power of Christ may dwell in me" (2 Cor. 12:9).

4. Short accounts are essential.

Scripture urges us to deal with issues as they arise, not to let the sun go down on our anger. When we sleep on an offense, it seems to grow bigger in the night. To obey God, we have no choice but to keep short accounts.

Lewis Smedes writes, "When you forgive someone for hurting you, you perform spiritual surgery inside your soul; you cut away the wrong that was done to you....Detach that person from the hurt and let it go, the way a child opens his hands and lets a trapped butterfly go free.

"Then invite that person back into your mind, fresh, as if a piece of history between you had been rewritten, its grip on your memory broken. Reverse the seemingly irreversible flow of pain within you."[9]

FOUR STEPS TO FORGIVENESS

In my experience as a teacher and counselor, I've found the following steps essential to forgiveness.

1. Prepare the heart.

In the same way that farmers plow the ground in preparation for planting seeds, we prepare our hearts to plant seeds of forgiveness. The essential first step in forgiveness is to spend time before the Lord in prayerful examination. Two passages for meditation are: "Test me, O LORD, and try me, examine my heart and my mind; for your love is ever before me, and I walk continually in your truth" (Ps. 26:2–3 NIV); and "Search me, O God, and know my heart; test me and know my anxious thoughts. See if there is any offensive way in me, and lead me in the way everlasting" (Ps. 139:23–24 NIV).

2. Let go of the hurt, bitterness, hatred, resentment.

By an act of the will, turn loose of the emotions bottled up inside. Whatever is physically, emotionally, mentally, or spiritually handicapping you, hand it over to the Lord. He is responding with mercy and grace. What is your part? Let the pot drop!

3. Ask God to teach you what you need to learn through it all.

Perhaps God wants to reveal your selfishness, a spirit of unbrokenness, increase your level of sensitivity, or give an advanced lesson in servanthood. If you maintain a teachable spirit during the difficult times, the experience will not be wasted. I've found this true in my own life.

4. Add your offender to your prayer list.

As we pray for those who have hurt us, we begin to see them as human beings with needs and hurts, too. Healing will come as we pray for them.

MAKING THE CHOICE TO FORGIVE

Three examples at the beginning of the chapter demonstrate the strong emotional tug toward bitterness when adversity strikes. However, in each situation, the offended person made a choice to forgive.

After his initial anguish, Dr. Upp learned more about the two teens who caused the death of his daughter. In a face-to-face encounter with Dr. Upp, the remorseful boys vowed they had never planned to hurt anyone. In their youthful exuberance, they did not weigh the consequences of their actions.

Somehow the compassion that Dr. Upp exercised daily as a pediatrician took hold in this situation. Later, Dr. Upp took his other daughter's hand and said, "God wants us to forgive these boys. That's what Diane would have wanted." Dr. Upp urged the court to consider rehabilitation over punishment.

The boys pled guilty and the judge issued a just sentence of two years in prison and seven years' probation for what they had done. Dr. Upp prays for them every day.

He said, "With His love, I was able to let go of the anger I carried against those boys and replace it with forgiveness. Vengeance wouldn't bring Diane back, but by showing God's infinite compassion, just as she had done, we would keep her spirit alive.

Diane is still spreading God's love on this earth. In that I find peace."[10]

What happened to Alex and Dorothea? They severed their relationship. But in the quietness of their separation, they each began self-examination, realizing they were each blaming the other for their problems instead of working them out. Fourteen months into their divorce, they were forced to talk to each other because of some unresolved tax questions.

At first they were defensive, but in time they began talking about other areas of their lives. Finally, they realized that the more they saw each other, the more they wanted to be together. They had changed. Each had become more compassionate and interested in the partner's welfare.

So they decided to get married again! Through their experiences, Alex and Dorothea learned what it means to forgive. Alex recalls, "We had hurt each other very badly through those twenty-eight years. Until we offered each other forgiveness, we really couldn't even start talking."

Dorothea admits, "I thought I couldn't forgive because I would be telling him it was OK to hurt me. And then I realized that forgiveness didn't mean it was OK: it only meant that I was going to let God handle it."

What is Alex's advice to couples in marital distress? "Don't give up! It's all right if you need some time apart, but stand fast, be patient, and don't give up!"[11]

It seems almost impossible that David Kiel, shot in the back by an irate customer could forgive. After all, David was now paralyzed, a quadriplegic, adjusting to life in a wheelchair. After leaving the rehabilitation center, David's attitude deteriorated as he endured physical pain and self-pity. He admits, "Bitterness was poisoning my soul. It was separating me from God. I would have to forgive the man who shot me. But I couldn't do it. I really didn't want to.

"I prayed many times in the weeks and months that followed. I forced myself to pray for that man. As I did, a degree of compassion for him grew within me. Though I was severely handicapped, I had Jesus to lean upon. The man who shot me probably did not. My attitude began to improve."

However, David was unable to save his marriage. His wife divorced him, gained custody of their children, and left David alone. She remarried and prospered financially while he was unable to find a job.

Then David struggled with bitterness toward his wife. When a Christian friend confronted him, David admitted his resentment. "Forgiveness was a real struggle for me. I couldn't seem to do it on my own. I had to depend on the Lord Jesus Christ to change my heart. And he did this through time and His Word."

The circumstances did not change, but David's attitude improved as he began investing himself in other people's lives. He shifted his focus from what was done to him to what he could do for Jesus. He now says, "I know that bitterness is something I simply cannot afford to have in my life. I want to make every moment count for Jesus Christ."[12]

THE BIG PAY-OFF: THE RESULTS OF FORGIVENESS

When we choose to forgive, we experience at least four positive results:

1. Fellowship—It is impossible to live in disobedience and walk in fellowship with God. You can't have it both ways. Sin breaks fellowship. On the other hand, when we've confessed known sin, it is a joy to wake up in the morning with, "Good morning, Lord!" because we sense His smile.

2. Freedom—Bitterness is like being in a prison made of our own grudges, guilt, and anger. When we forgive, the prison bars are broken! Personal freedom reigns.

3. Future—Not asking, "Why, God?" but rather asking, "How, God?"—How can I get on with my life from here?—will keep us looking ahead. As Paul admonishes us, "Forgetting what lies behind and reaching forward to what lies ahead, I press on toward the goal for the prize of the upward call of God in Christ Jesus" (Phil. 3:13–14).

4. Fruitfulness—The farmer knows it's impossible to harvest a healthy crop if weeds are allowed to dominate the field. Likewise, the Christian who wants to bear the fruit of a spirit-filled life eliminates bitterness before it takes root. Forgiveness is appropriate anytime an offense occurs. The quicker, the better.

Old habits are hard to break and some people get in a pattern of responding to life's bumps and blows with bitterness. While it may seem impossible to change, it's not. We can learn new disciplines, keep promises, be faithful to our vows, and become genuinely considerate of others' feelings and convictions. The task ahead is never greater than the power behind so we can lock arms with Paul in saying, "I can do all things through Him who strengthens me" (Phil. 4:13).

CHAPTER TWELVE

Building Fences

Don't let the world around you squeeze you into its own mold, but let God remold your minds from within.

ROMANS 12:2 PHILLIPS

Twenty-four years ago, I struggled with a difficult situation. I'd been out of seminary thirteen years and was abruptly unemployed, not by choice. With our three older kids ready for college—no money, and no place to live—my back was against the wall. Or so I thought. I was ready to quit the ministry to sell insurance or used cars—whatever it would take to keep my family out of the financial hole.

Then Pearl came to me with some notes she had written after prolonged prayer—notes which detailed her thoughts for a Bible-teaching ministry. I still remember reading Pearl's notes and considering all the changes that would be involved. Then with tear-filled eyes I prayed, "Lord, if this is what You want, we'll go for it."

We did. As we began our teaching and traveling ministry I prayed, "Oh, God, make me a man with a burning heart, busy hands, and bloody feet. I must go where they are and bring them the Word."

Consequently, through the years we've seen the Lord faithfully provide the educational needs for our five children. Some have even earned graduate degrees! Yet, if we had done what seemed expedient to me at the time, we would have missed a rich harvest of spiritual blessings.

Although I knew Christ had called me into the ministry, the crisis tempted me to look in other directions. The lure to forsake Christ's call upon each of our lives is not new. When crunch time came for Judas, he took the money and bailed out in betrayal of Jesus. Demas, one of Paul's coworkers, jumped ship, forsaking the apostle and the work "having loved this present world" (2 Tim. 4:10).

In considering the pull of today's society upon each of us, what can we do to maintain our commitment to Christ?

CONFORMITY OR COMMITMENT?

In farm areas, fences are used to mark boundaries, to keep animals in, and to protect valuable crops from destruction by roaming beasts. While barbed wire is often the choice on western cattle ranges, post and rail, picket fences, woven wire, and a variety of others are common in various settings. I prefer electric fences. They let you know they're there when you bump into them. The main characteristic of a fence is that it separates.

Satan accuses God of protecting Job and all his belongings with a thornbush fence. "Have you not put a hedge around him and his household and everything he has? You have blessed the work of his hands, so that his flocks and herds are spread throughout the land" (Job 1:10 NIV).

When we fall in love with the one we marry, we start building fences of separation. Sheldon Vanauken in his book, *A Severe Mercy,* calls it "our shining barrier:"

This present glory, love once-given grace,
The sum of blessing in a sure embrace,

Must not in creeping separateness decline
But be the centre of our whole design...

This splendor is upon us, high and pure,
As heaven: and we swear it shall endure:
Swear fortitude for pain and faith for tears
To hold our shining barrier down the years."[1]

Paul says a similar thing about his relationship to the Lord in 2 Corinthians 5:14. I like to read it as: "For the love of Christ is holding me within its bounds." When we come to know the Lord Jesus as Savior we enter into a love relationship with Him and we are His. He doesn't take lightly anybody trespassing on His property. Woe to anyone who touches the apple of His eye.

But the problem isn't others so much as it is us. We take down the fences and begin roaming the range. When I was in high school, I remember a song the Andrews sisters sang along with Bing Crosby called "Don't Fence Me In." It talks of a cowboy riding alone in the open country, gazing at the stars and listening to the breeze blowing through the trees. His main request? Freedom. He says, "Don't fence me in." That sure sounds like a song for the 90s, doesn't it?

We believers are in the world but not of the world. God's "fences" are the commands and principles of His Word. Our spiritual health depends upon our staying within the boundaries He defines. As we rely upon the grace of our Shepherd, the Lord Jesus Christ, we have everything we need. We graze in His green pastures, and drink from His springs of living water.

Rod Sargent writes, "Holiness is not a list of universally approved do's and don'ts. Rather it is separation to God, and from the ungodly, the ordinary, and the common. Our greatest danger as Christians usually lies not in profane acts, but in allowing common daily activities to crowd Christ out of our lives."[2] We look for holes in our Father's fences. When we go astray we end up in the far country.

In other words, if we are not separated from the value system of the world, we lose our testimony for Jesus Christ. James is strong here: "You adulteresses, do you not know that friendship with the world is hostility toward God? Therefore whoever wishes to be a friend of the world makes himself an enemy of God" (James 4:4).

While we may not all be pastors, each of us is called to commitment. Often we are tempted, however, to sit on the fence and keep one foot in the world and one foot with Christ. He says, "No one can serve two masters; for either he will hate the one and love the other, or he will hold to one and despise the other. You cannot serve God and Mammon" (Matt. 6:24).

BIBLICAL AND MODERN EXAMPLES

Elkanah is a biblical example of a man characterized by concessions, conformity, and compromises. He adopted the culturally acceptable practice in his day and lived with two wives, Peninnah and Hannah.

His religious experience was superficial and primarily selfish. He went to the temple and made yearly sacrifices because it looked good. It was the thing to do. Elkanah never plumbed the depths of God's grace. He was living apart from God's ideal, divine plan for marriage—one husband, one wife for life.

Like Elkanah, some of us make conscious choices to go against what the Scriptures clearly teach. We rationalize our behaviors and lifestyles and make excuses for sin. Instead of separating ourselves from the world, we just let it squeeze us into its mold.

A few years ago when Joe's business came crashing down, he

became soft and tender toward God and His Word. He shared Scripture, memorized verses, and testified of his faith to others. But when the crisis passed, his attitude changed.

Now getting him into an accountability group to help him deal with personal issues is like trying to pull a jackass into the barn when he doesn't want to go. Joe doesn't seem to need the Lord anymore. He is "doing fine" without Him.

Scripture warns, "Do not love the world nor the things in the world. If any one loves the world, the love of the Father is not in him. For all that is in the world, the lust of the flesh and the lust of the eyes and the boastful pride of life, is not from the Father, but is from the world. And the world is passing away, and also its lusts; but the one who does the will of God abides forever" (1 John 2:15–17).

One of Elkanah's wives, Peninnah, as I see her, was probably hedonistic, a lover of pleasure. Lifted from the Old Testament pages and placed in modern America, we'd probably find her consumed with the latest fashion trends, driving a Mercedes, wearing expensive jewelry, eating at the health-food store, sipping Perrier, and spending hours at the beauty shop with her nose in *Cosmopolitan.*

From the biblical account Peninnah was a sarcastic, scornful, selfish woman, envious and jealous of Elkanah's other wife, Hannah. Scripture does not mention that Peninnah ever called upon the Lord.

In marked contrast, Hannah had a genuine heart for God. She was a servant, committed to the Lord and confident in Him. However, she remained childless while Peninnah had children. Hannah went to the temple where she earnestly prayed for a son and promised the Lord that if He saw fit to answer her prayer, she would dedicate her son to His service. "Elkanah lay with Hannah his wife, and the LORD remembered her" (1 Sam. 1:19 NIV).

After her son, Samuel, was born and weaned, Hannah kept her promise and took him back to the temple where she told Eli the priest, " 'I prayed for this child, and the LORD has granted me what I asked of him. So now I give him to the LORD. For his whole life he will be given over to the LORD.' And he worshiped the LORD there" (1 Sam. 1:27–28 NIV). Then Hannah worshiped and praised God with joy.

Like Naomi and Ruth before her, Hannah makes difficult choices in a contrary culture. She beautifully demonstrates not only the Lord's provision, but His protection and His blessing upon her as she is faithful to Him.

COMMITMENT—NOT JUST FOR THE YOUNG

Eli, the temple priest was not a great man like Moses or Aaron, but his ambition drove him to assume the roles of both. Results? Eli failed both as a priest and as a parent. His carelessness, carnality, and complacency finally led to the collapse of his family and his ministry. We might say Eli was a religious leader suffering from burnout.

As a result, he abdicated his responsibilities as a parent. He abandoned and failed to lead his family. His sons are described as "wicked men; they had no regard for the LORD" (1 Sam. 2:12 NIV).

In addition, Eli quit taking care of his own physical needs as he continually sat. Maybe he was the first couch potato! As the late coach Vince Lombardi said, "Fatigue makes cowards of us all."

In the end, weariness left Eli without drive or incentive. With no motivation to keep going, he became careless and sloppy. He just sat, ate, and finally fell over backward out of his chair, breaking his neck on impact. He died a fat, frustrated, frumpy failure.

Scripture paints vivid portraits of others who failed to finish well. Other men occupying the Hall of Shame are Lot, Gideon, Samson, Nadab, Abihu, Gehazi, Asa, Saul, Solomon, Hezekiah, and Judas, just to name a few!

Today our culture plays well into the scenario by focusing on retirement, telling us that significant activity and productivity cease in our sixties and seventies. Not true. Life should intensify and become fuller as we anticipate seeing the One who would rather die than live without us, the One we have lived for and longed for throughout our Christian experience.

SECURING THE FENCE

Meanwhile, back at the farm—remember the old conversation between a pig and a chicken? The chicken suggests serving the farmer a breakfast of eggs and bacon in appreciation for his kindness. The pig's answer is classic: "Sure, that's easy for you to say. What you're giving is a gift and what I'm giving is total commitment."

What the Lord Jesus Christ is asking for is total commitment. He wants us in for the long-haul. The Christian life is no Caribbean cruise to port Glory but a trail slick and sloppy with struggle and sacrifice. We can never doubt that salvation is a free gift of God's grace, but to quote John Denver: "Life ain't no easy freeway, there's some gravel on the ground." Perhaps we should remind ourselves that our focus is upon Christ.

Pearl and I were in our first year of seminary in January of 1956 when we heard of missionary Jim Elliot's disappearance. He and four other bright young men, the cream of the crop, were attempting to establish a remote mission outpost among the Auca Indians, an Ecuadorian tribe known to kill indiscriminately. Only days before, the men had flown into the area and transmitted news of limited contact with the tribe. Now the radio was silent.

Our prayer vigil continued as tensions mounted. Since Pearl had known one of the missionaries, Roger Youderian, as a fellow-student at Northwestern College, we felt a close kinship with the missing men.

However, apprehension turned to horror as a reconnaissance party discovered the young men slain by spears and arrows on the beach in Auca territory. Evidently, the missionaries had chosen not to resist the attack, nor to injure their Auca killers. The revolvers which might have protected them were left unfired.

At a later time when Jim Elliot's widow, Elisabeth, and pilot Nate Saint's sister, Rachel, returned to the territory, the Aucas learned about Christ and His forgiveness. One of the killers was subsequently converted when he learned the missionaries could have mounted armed resistance, but chose to let their guns remain silent.

Jim Elliot had written years earlier in his devotional diary: "He is no fool who gives what he cannot keep to gain what he cannot lose" and "Blood is only of value as it flows before Thine altar."[3]

Sometimes the cost of commitment is exceedingly high. But is this unexpected when we are committed to a Leader who has experienced the same? Why should we be surprised by what appears to be premature departures from this earth? From the Sovereign Father's perspective, the men's work was done.

While our Christian commitment may not be tested to the degree of these men and while we may not be martyred for our faith, many Christians throughout history have been. They remained true to the end. The question is—Will we?

A MARRIAGE COMMITMENT

A commitment in marriage is really a picture of our commitment to Jesus Christ. I don't remember contemplating the cost involved in my marriage commitment on August 14, 1953. Nor do I recall wincing at the price to be paid in future years as we would hammer out our differences to bring about oneness. I hadn't a clue. I only knew I loved Pearl and wanted to spend the rest of my life with her. We recently celebrated our forty-third anniversary.

Just as we made a covenant with God to stay together, we also made a commitment to nurture and teach our children and grandchildren about Him. We have entrusted our finances to Him as well. In other words, He owns us lock, stock, and barrel. We are in good hands! My rendition of 1 Thessalonians 5:24 is "Faithful is the one who is calling you, who also will do it."

IS THE GRASS REALLY GREENER ON THE OTHER SIDE?

When driving down Texas highways I often see a cow poking its head through a barbed-wire fence and munching grass on the other side. Why do cows do that? Is it curiosity or a lack of contentment with provisions in the pasture? I don't know. I sure do know a lot of people who are living like that.

Many fail to understand that God's fences are for our benefit. Just as obedience to God's principles yields the fruit of peace and blessing, disobedience yields bitter consequences. Since the beginning of time, man has challenged the moral laws of God and tried to jump the fence. Instead of feeding on God's Word and obeying His precepts, some have gazed at the world's pasture and found it appealing. Yet many biblical examples demonstrate the devastating results of wrong choices.

David got his eyes on the lady next door and put his head through the fence. The Lord confronted him with these sobering words through Nathan, the prophet; "And if all this had been too little, I would have given you even more. Why did you despise the word of the LORD by doing what is evil in his eyes?" (2 Sam. 12:8–9 NIV). Ouch!

Lot—When Abraham gave Lot a homestead choice, he put the binoculars on the well-watered plains of Jordan. Consequently, he, Mrs. Lot, and their family became residents of the homosexual capitals of the world: Sodom and Gomorrah (Gen. 13:10–13).

King Saul—King Saul became impatient, took matters into his own hands, and offered a sacrifice instead of waiting for the priest according to the law. Consequently, he lost his kingdom. Saul's disobedience led to his downfall (1 Sam. 13:8–9, 15:22–23).

Gehazi—Gehazi, the servant, chased the chariot of Naaman. When Naaman stopped and addressed his need, he requested gifts for the sons of the prophets. He took the gifts, but instead of giving them away, he hid the gifts in his house and lied about it. Elisha the prophet exposed his greedy, evil deed and Gehazi lost his job and became leprous (2 Kings 5:20–27).

Rich young ruler—Jesus challenged the rich young ruler to sell all his possessions and give them to the poor because Jesus knew that while the young man tried to keep the Old Testament laws, he had made an idol of his possessions. The rich young ruler turned away from Jesus because he owned much and couldn't bring himself to part with it (Mark 10:17–22).

In my office I have a beautiful picture of a large rainbow trout poised to strike a fly that has just fallen in front of him with a line attached. You can tell the fish is focused, enticed, hungry, and ready. He has already made his choice. In a similar way, Satan dangled the fruit before Eve and she took it. The Devil's been enticing us for years and with total disregard for the Father's restraints. Before we know it—wham! He's allured another one. You can almost hear him saying: "Gotcha!"

Karl Menninger said: "When a trout rising to a fly gets hooked on a line and finds himself unable to swim about freely, he begins with a fight which results in struggles and splashes and sometimes an escape. Often, of course, the situation is too tough for him."[4]

James 1:13–16 also uses fishing language to describe the process. My interpretation is: "Let no man say when he is being tempted, 'I am being tempted by God'; for God cannot be tempted to do evil, and He Himself is tempting no one. But each one is being tempted when he is taken in tow and lured by his own desires. Then when the desire has conceived, it is giving birth to sin; and this sin when it has run its course, brings forth death. Stop being deceived, my brethren, beloved ones."

Choices, choices, choices. When we act in disobedience to God's standards, we have just saddled a dead horse. The greener grass is an illusion. Right choices may not always be easy, but they are vital for people who love God and want to honor Him in our world today.

Confronted with the crisis of continuing to choose correctly, we can give in, give out, give up, or go on. For those of us who feel both beat up and bedraggled, Scripture holds a promise, "But those who hope in the LORD will renew their strength. They will soar on wings like eagles; they will run and not grow weary, they will walk and not be faint" (Is. 40:31 NIV).

FENCING OUT THE ROAMING BEASTS

It is easy to underestimate the power of the adversary in the Christian walk. Quite often the greatest enemy lies within. Before a new Christian can make progress, he needs to identify several hindrances. Here are a few temptations we all face:

The Past

Someone has said—When the past quarrels with the present there can be no future. The Bible teaches us to lay aside our regrets and guilt and get on with the business of serving God. As Samuel tells the nation of Israel, "Do not be afraid. You have done all this evil; yet do not turn away from the LORD, but serve the LORD with all your heart" (1 Sam. 12:20 NIV).

The apostle Paul himself was no stranger to past failure. "Brethren, I do not regard myself as having laid hold of it yet; but one thing I do: forgetting what lies behind and reaching forward to what lies ahead" (Phil. 3:13). Like Paul, we choose to let go of the past.

When we become Christians each of us carries into our new family of God a private past, some of which we may feel ashamed about and some over which we had no control. Perhaps we deeply regret the awful insensitivity with which we have responded to others. I know how that feels.

Several years ago I lost a special partner in ministry. He had touched thousands of lives for Christ over his many years of service. God used him tremendously. While in his office, I remember reading a framed tribute written by his daughter in honor and gratitude for her dad's life, ministry, and example.

Two hours after I had been visiting with him one day, he tragically took his own life. Thoughts began to haunt me. Had I failed to be sensitive to his silent pain? Was I really listening to him? What if I had handed him a little note? Or told him how I felt about him and his contributions? Would it have made a difference? Would he still be bearing fruit for God's glory today if I had sensed his need? And what about his family? Are they remembering him with a grateful heart?

Yes, when we become Christians we are new creations and the old things are passed away. The power of sin is broken and Satan is a defeated foe. But he can still use unresolved areas in our lives to establish a base of operations to wreak havoc within.

When we come to Christ, most of us do come with a load of emotional baggage. We need to deal with it. Forgiving ourselves and others is a vital part of leaving the past behind.

Disobedience

Moses warned the Israelites, "Be careful that you do not forget the LORD your God, failing to observe his commands, his laws, and his decrees that I am giving you this day" (Deut. 8:11 NIV).

Knowing God is in the business of blessing the obedient heart, Moses again cautions the people, "Now what I am commanding you today is not too difficult for you or beyond your reach...No, the word is very near you; it is in your mouth and in your heart so you may obey it" (Deut. 30:11, 14 NIV).

The children of Israel go into the land under Joshua's leadership and make all these wonderful statements of committed obedience at the end of his life and when we open the Book of Judges, the most oft repeated phrase is: "Again the Israelites did evil in the eyes of the LORD" (Judg. 13:1 NIV).

Pride

We are often tempted to become proud in times of prosperity. Moses mentions five signs of material abundance.

1. The Israelites will eat and be satisfied.
2. They will build good houses and live in them.
3. Their herds and flocks will multiply.
4. Their silver and gold will multiply.
5. All they have will multiply.

Prosperity is dangerous when we fail to realize its source and when we place more faith in the wealth than in the One who provided our needs. Moses adds one sober warning about what may happen in a land of plenty. "You may say to yourself, 'My power and the strength of my hands have produced this wealth for me'" (Deut. 8:17 NIV).

Jesus told a parable of a wealthy CEO who prepared for early retirement by stockpiling his wealth. God issued a sober reminder of who was truly in charge. "And I will say to my soul, 'Soul, you have many goods laid up for many years to come; take your ease, eat, drink and be merry.' But God said to him, 'You fool! This very night your soul is required of you; and now who will own what you have prepared?'" (Luke 12:19–20).

One of my passions for ministry is Christian camping. We have been looking for several years at Colorado properties. One of these properties is called Tom Cat Ranch. What a place! Everything is state of the art. Electronic gates, exotic quarters, vaulted ceilings, weightroom, hot tub. Everything is lavishly overdone and waiting for the owner to move in. I then heard this story from the realtor.

Tom was very successful. He and his wife drew up these plans for an eight-thousand-square-foot mansion to be their dwelling place for the rest of their lives. Everything was finished and they were ready to take possession on February 1, but they never had that opportunity. Both died in a plane crash the night before they were to move into their new home. What a graphic picture of earthly goods left behind.

Ungratefulness

When difficulties arise we sometimes forget what God has done for us in the past. Forgetfulness isn't a unique temptation. Paul challenges the Ephesians to remember God who brought them into union with Him (Eph. 2:11–12). Jesus understood the shortness of human memory, so He took the bread and the cup and instituted the Lord's Supper, telling us to take part in remembrance of Him (Luke 22:17–20).

Likewise Moses reminds the people of God's goodness to them, calling them to remember that God brought them out from the land of Egypt, out of the house of slavery, and led them through the great and terrible wilderness. During their wanderings, God provided water and food, and protected them from serpents and scorpions (Deut. 8:14–16). God did all this in the past, in Moses' words, "to humble and to test you so that in the end it might go well with you" (Deut. 8:16, NIV).

Luke tells us that Jesus healed ten lepers who requested it. "Now one of them, when he saw that he had been healed, turned back, glorifying God with a loud voice, and he fell on his face at His feet, giving thanks to Him. And he was a Samaritan. And Jesus answered and said, 'Were there not ten cleansed? But the nine—where are they?'" (Luke 17:15–17).

Gratitude is an attitude! Patriotism is a form of gratitude. I am reminded of what it cost in shed blood for me to live in a free country. If those who died were on parade, the line would circle the globe.

Gratitude is also the oil in the machinery of interpersonal relationships. At our spring couples' conferences this year, I had participants write a tribute after each of the four sessions.

In the first session they wrote a tribute to their mates.
In the second session they wrote a tribute to their children.
In the third session they wrote a tribute to their parents.
In the fourth session they wrote a tribute to God.

That exercise gave those attending a renewed appreciation for one another and for God.

Independence

Another roaming beast we want to fence out is a spirit of independence. If we do not learn dependence upon God, we may end up with a hip out of joint like Jacob. We will be making the rest of the trip leaning on the top of a staff. We can be so stubborn and bull-headed at times. God then must take us through the breaking process.

Scott and Janina Walker are hosts for one of my home Bible

studies. I was touched one evening as Scott shared his testimony: "At age thirty-eight my life was out of control. I was drinking heavily. My marriage and my employment were in jeopardy. Midlife transition was rapidly becoming midlife crisis. I never studied God's Word and seldom prayed. When I did pray, it was mostly the 911 type. I had abdicated my role as the spiritual leader of my family.

"I knew the Lord had been knocking on my heart's door for many years, but I stubbornly refused to respond. Instead, I attended church, occasionally dropped money in the offering plate, contributed to worthy community causes, and patted myself on the back for being a better husband and father than most other guys I knew.

"Outwardly, I was cruising along thinking I was a pretty neat guy because of my achievements. My athletic abilities had paid for my undergraduate and graduate education, and my business skills had landed some great employment opportunities. My wife, son, and daughter were in good health. Any onlooker would think I had it made.

"But inwardly my life had jumped the tracks. My marriage relationship with Janina was deteriorating. Soon I became restless and discontented with my job. Pride and selfishness were pushing me to the breaking point.

"Then six years ago, in my hour of deepest need, another couple invitied Janina and me to attend Don Anderson's Bible study in a nearby home. Janina had already sensed a spiritual void in her life and she really wanted to go. After she kept prodding me, I finally but reluctantly said, "Well, I'll go with you just once."

"At first I thought, *Why should I go to a Bible study? I haven't done anything bad—like murder, rape, or robbery. I'm a good guy.* Although I agreed to attend just to placate my wife, little did I know that God was planning a divine appointment with me.

"That night the Lord began showing me I was living in spiritual darkness. Again, I felt Him knocking at my heart's door. Right then with some fear and trepidation, I opened it. Through God's Word I began to see myself as a sinner in need of a Savior. What a difference Jesus Christ began to make in my life! By God's grace I am a new creation.

"My personal encounter with Christ has revolutionized my home and my work. All the energy I once expended in resisting Him is now focused on pursuing Him and His will by the reading of His Word."

Scott's story reminds me of David's words, "The sacrifices of God are a broken spirit; a broken and contrite heart, O God, you will not despise" (Ps. 51:17 NIV).

Hannah Hurnard, in her little book *Mountain of Spices,* puts it this way:

In acceptance lieth peace,
    O my heart be still;
Let thy restless worries cease
    And accept his will.
Though this test be not thy choice,
    It is his—therefore rejoice.

In his plan there cannot be
    Ought to make thee sad:
If this is his choice for thee,
    Take it and be glad.
Make from it some lovely thing
    To the glory of thy King.
Cease from sighs and murmurings,
    Sing his loving grace,

This thing means thy furthering
To a wealthy place
From thy fears he'll give release,
In acceptance lieth peace."[5]

THE GATE

Just as we want to be aware of the temptations of attitude and heart, we need a target, a goal, a positive incentive. Someone once asked a farmer how he won a plowing contest. His answer? "I fixed my eyes on a tree at the end of the row."

We might think of life like plowing. At the end of the row is our model, Jesus Christ. The question is—Are we looking unto Jesus? Are we focused on Him? Perhaps we have our binoculars on the well-watered plains of Jordan. Do we find ourselves focusing on the temporary life? What are we viewing?

Stability in our Christian walk increases only as we choose to be humble, dependent upon God, grateful, and obedient. Just as a farmer builds fences on his farm, we implement Scripture under the direction of the Holy Spirit to give us a sense of direction and boundaries. As believers, we understand that irritations of life are opportunities to practice applying scriptural principles. Overcoming temptations strengthens us to remain steadfast in the faith.

As we implement biblical truth to various circumstances, we nurture our inner being. When decisions and choices come, we are then able to reach in and draw upon wisdom and discernment through Christ. Riches and the things of this world lose their importance.

A fence begins and ends with a gate. The Lord Jesus is that gate. Hear Him as He nears the end of the Sermon on the Mount: "Enter by the narrow gate; for the gate is wide, and the way is broad that leads to destruction, and many are those who enter by it. For the gate is small, and the way is narrow that leads to life, and few are those who find it" (Matt. 7:13–14).

Chapter Thirteen

Staying Steady in the Storm

For I consider that the sufferings of this present time are not worthy to be compared with the glory that is to be revealed to us.

Romans 8:18

Occasionally a comedian can get serious. Once I heard humorist Grady Nutt relate the story of how a tornado ripped through his city. The morning after the devastating storm, Grady and his wife headed for the home of some friends. They hoped their friends' house had been spared, although news reports indicated the twister had plunged right through their neighborhood.

But when the Nutts arrived, they found the residence in shambles. The yard and driveway were filled with debris; a large tree had crushed the garage. They waded through rubble just to reach the front porch and then were unable to open the door. When they climbed through a living room window and called for their friends, a noise from the stairway caught their attention. As they looked up, a broad shaft of sunlight streaming down from above illuminated the dear wife. Holding a muddy chandelier and looking for all the world like the goddess of justice with scales in her hand, she said simply, "We're okay, Grady. We just lost a house." Grady's friends had lost a house but not their perspective.

Tornadoes can be devastating. That's why farmers keep an eye on the weather, and when the black clouds roll in, many farmers secure their equipment and head for the storm cellar.

The forces of nature can hamper and even destroy potential crops. Freezing temperatures at the wrong time can ruin a fruit harvest; and a drought can make hay a scarce commodity. Both scenarios are distressing.

Likewise, in the Christian life, we often experience various kinds of adversity. How can we handle it? Where can we go? What can we do?

SUFFERING IS INEVITABLE

As members of the fallen human race, we will experience the tragedies of life. So the question is not *if* the storms will hit, but *when*. Peter writes about this in 1 Peter 4:12–13. I think he is saying, "Beloved, do not be surprised at the fiery ordeal which is coming upon you, as though something strange were happening to you; but inasmuch as you are sharing the sufferings of Christ, be rejoicing; in order that also at the revelation of His glory, you might shout for joy."

After becoming a Christian, Paul goes through one ordeal after another. What a trail of tears this man travels! Before he can even get out of Damascus as a new believer, Jews plot against him. He is rescued by fellow believers who, under the cover of darkness, let him down through a hole in the city wall by ropes tied to a basket. Others are afraid of him because of his reputation. Paul is sentenced to receive thirty-nine lashes on five different occasions. Three times he is beaten with rods. Once he is stoned and left for dead.

Shipwrecks, robbers, riots, verbal and physical abuse all take their toll, but his attitude remains firm as he says, "We are handicapped on all sides, but we are never frustrated; we are puzzled, but never in despair. We are persecuted, but we never have to stand it alone: we may be knocked down but we are never knocked out!" (2 Cor. 4:8–9 PHILLIPS).

Peter affirms Paul's perspective by saying: "For you have been called for this purpose, since Christ also suffered for you leaving you an example for you to follow in His steps" (1 Peter 2:21). Paul knows he is being made more like Jesus Christ as he shares in the fellowship of His suffering. That makes it all worthwhile.

"This is the reason why we never collapse. The outward man does indeed suffer wear and tear, but every day the inward man receives fresh strength. These little troubles (which are really so transitory) are winning for us a permanent, glorious and solid reward out of all proportion to our pain" (2 Cor. 4:16–17 PHILLIPS).

My precious Pearl paints the graphic picture of the way it all happens:

> Ah, suffering my painful friend;
> you take the bubble of comfort
> I have so carefully built around myself
> and in a seemingly cruel fashion
> snatch it from my clinging hands
> and dash it to the ground;
> where it breaks into a hundred pieces
> and leaves me exposed and trembling.
> Again, I must take the choice:
> Do I retreat or do I move on?[1]

How can we hang in there and keep plowing through the trials and testing of our lives today? Some of us have lost our jobs, our spouses through death or divorce, our children through death, drugs, or physical and emotional separation. Some of us have lost our health and our zeal for living. What can we do when the storms of life whip us about? Here are insights I have found helpful.

PRINCIPLES FOR STAYING STEADY

Keep the Joy

Difficulties do not come into our lives because the Lord is unhappy with us but because He wants, through these experiences, to help us grow toward spiritual maturity. Often when problems slam us against the wall, we pray, "Lord, change my circumstances!" What He really wants is to change us to meet those circumstances. We see opposition, but He sees opportunity.

Staying joyful in devastating circumstances does not mean grinning like a Cheshire cat when the cancer scan is positive, the prognosis dim, and the children neglectful or rebellious. It is not, "Praise God! My husband is leaving me for a younger woman, and I'll get to raise these six kids all by myself!" It is not, "Oh, goody! I lost my job!" It is not some phony baloney spiritual happiness complete with a pleasant robotic mask and a refusal to feel or to admit pain. Sometimes life hurts—Big time! Denial is not part of the plan, but joy is.

Keeping the joy means:

- choosing proactively to trust God with the situation and learn from it.
- staying confident in His ability to handle everything.
- manifesting through His strength that inner peace, courageous character, and quiet confidence that He will see us through.
- realizing what is vitally important and what is not.

My dear friend, John Mackinnon, demonstrated how to traverse life's peaks and valleys. Stricken in midlife with Lou Gehrig's Disease, he dealt with us honestly. He saturated himself with God's truth, a lifelong habit for him; and then he met the new physical and emotional challenges with candor, character, and confidence in God. He tenaciously hung onto life until God called him home. John remained joyful as he departed for Heaven's gates. Although he is no longer on earth, John's remembrance remains an inspiration to us all. He never lost his joy.

Ask for Help

Pearl grew up on a farm in Oklahoma. As a young girl she'd heard that a goose would stay on her nest and protect it to the death. One afternoon while doing chores, Pearl decided to test the theory. So she took a stick and started jabbing and swiping at the sitting goose. Sure enough the goose stayed, but it also began a series of hissing and honking sounds. Pearl didn't know the hissing was a warning to her while the goose's honking was a distress signal to her gander-mate. Within seconds Pearl heard a noise behind her. As she quickly turned, the gander, his wings spread and claws three inches off the ground, approached with a vengeance. Terrified, Pearl locked eyes with the advancing bird, started swinging her stick wildly, and began retreating step by step. Suddenly, Pearl's legs hit a calf trough filled with water. Her momentum carried her backwards, and down she plopped with a huge splash!

Pearl's yell of fear and surprise stopped the gander in midflight and also brought her brother running from his task. He laughed at the scene and delighted in telling the story at supper that evening. I didn't know her then, but my sweet bride gained some wisdom that day while in a tub with her feet up in the air!

All of us can identify with finding out some things the hard way, but the Lord says if we need wisdom we can ask for help. "But if any of you lacks wisdom, let him ask of God, who gives to all men generously and without reproach, and it will be given to him" (James 1:5). God does not withhold or reserve wisdom when we request it.

Because our thoughts are not His thoughts and neither our ways His ways, we constantly need wisdom to know what God is trying to do in our lives. How do we grow and mature as a result of our difficulty? We inquire. He reveals. In His time and in His way. "He has made everything beautiful in its time..." (Eccles. 3:11 NIV).

Unfortunately though, instead of asking for discernment, we often start fighting to escape the pressure produced by the problem. What we often fail to realize is that by appealing to God, we are submitting. Then as we get our eyes off the circumstances and onto the Lord of the situation, things begin to change. "Trust in the LORD with all your heart and lean not on your own understanding; in all your ways acknowledge him, and he will make your paths straight" (Prov. 3:5–6 NIV).

Zodhiates in his commentary on James says, "Wisdom is necessary if we are to become masters of circumstances and not servants thereof. Unless there is within us that which is above us, we shall soon yield to that which is about us."[2]

Affirm God's Goodness

When stormy winds blow, Satan often tempts the child of God to doubt his Heavenly Father's goodness. How could God be good and permit such difficulty? The serpent snared Eve in the garden with this very strategy and these deceptive words: "You will not surely die...For God knows that when you eat of it your eyes will be opened, and you will be like God, knowing good and evil" (Gen. 3:4–5 NIV). Satan's ploy was to cause Adam and Eve to doubt God's goodness and His loving restraint in forbidding them to eat of the fruit of the tree. It worked. We are still reaping the bitter harvest of their rebellion today.

Regardless of our circumstances, it helps to use confidence when affirming and personalizing three realities about God:

Father, I know You love me.
Father, I know You will not permit circumstances that are not for my ultimate good.
Father, I can thank You for what You have allowed to happen in my life to this point.

God doesn't change. He's still in the business of saying, "Trust Me, I have everything under control." The better we get to know Him through Bible study, prayer, and constant companionship, the more we know that God is good. Our difficulties do not change the character of God, but they become opportunities for us to take refuge in His shelter of love. Even when we are puzzled by events, we know that His greatest desire is for our spiritual growth and development.

Focus on the Eternal

Our trials do not last forever. Life, wealth, poverty, and trouble are all temporary. The believer staying steady in the storm focuses on things eternal. But the temptation is to do otherwise.

We don't like waiting out the storm by waiting on God. If life isn't all downhill with the wind at our backs, we are tempted to look at worldly solutions to make the ride easier. Trouble with a colleague means we job-jump instead of getting to the root of the problem. Marital discord means seeking a new wife or husband instead of working things out. We may substitute material goals for spiritual ones when things get rough.

To guard against this danger Paul told the Corinthians: "For we are looking all the time not at the visible things but at the invisible. The visible things are transitory: it is the invisible things that are really permanent" (2 Cor. 4:18 PHILLIPS).

Remember, money doesn't buy love, happiness, or what it did last year. Paul writes to young Timothy saying, "Instruct those who are rich in this present world not to be conceited or to fix their hope on the uncertainty of riches, but on God, who richly supplies us with all things to enjoy" (1 Tim. 6:17).

I once heard a humorous story about giving. The church was having a congregational meeting in hopes of inspiring the saints to be generous in their contributions to the building program. One very wealthy parishioner stood up and said: "I think I can spare fifty dollars." When he sat down a piece of ceiling tile came loose and hit the old gentleman on the head. Sensing that the Lord had obviously spoken, he stood up again and said: "Make that one hundred dollars." One elderly saint prayed right out loud: "Lord! Hit him again!"

I think it was Jimmy Townsend who said: "When it comes to giving some folks will stop at nothing..."

Expect Reward

We often hear worldly things like "We only go around once in life." "Come along with me, the best is yet to be!" "It doesn't get any better than this!" But I say, "Oh yes, it does!" My interpretation of James 1:12 says, "Happy is the man who being tested is holding his ground; because, having been approved, he shall receive the crown of life, which He promised to those who love Him."

When we remain steadfast in the storm, we will receive a reward. "Be faithful until death and I will give you the crown of life" (Rev. 2:10). As we described in earlier chapters, the Lord will be recognizing winners and giving out trophies. This ought to motivate us to follow in His steps. We grow by solving our problems, not running away from them. We seek to endure, not to escape. Perseverance is the price for the Prize.

God is more concerned about developing within us the character of Christ than He is with making us comfortable. That is why we draw upon His grace when difficulties come. God is far more impressed with the fixed star than the flashing meteor. Our great example is Jesus Christ who is the same yesterday, today, and forever. He is constant, changeless, and will be there to lead us in triumph.

Job, in the Old Testament, was stripped by the storm that roared through his life. It claimed his possessions, and then a twister caused the death of his ten children. In the midst of heartache, Job affirmed his faith in God. "Naked I came from my mother's womb, and naked I will depart. The LORD gave and the LORD has taken away; may the name of the LORD be praised" (Job 1:21 NIV). Boom or Bust Lord! Like Job, I am Yours!

BENEFITS OF THE STORM

Farmers know that while boiling dark clouds often conceal unwanted winds, they also harbor the promise of rain. Without rain, most crops will fail to produce and stock ponds will disappear.

Likewise, as Christians we find the storms of life testing our place of refuge. Will we find security in our career? our salary? our title? Will we turn to something to dull the pain—Drugs? Alcohol? Promiscuity?

Or will we allow God to teach us, refine us, and purify us? When the disciples experienced a storm with Jesus in their boat, they called out to Him, beheld His face, and He became their Savior. As Max Lucado writes, "A season of suffering is a small price to pay for a clear view of God."[3]

Just as rain nourishes the soil, our spiritual lives are enriched by drawing closer to the Savior, the safest place to be. Hosea the prophet says it well; "Sow for yourselves righteousness, reap the fruit of unfailing love, and break up your unplowed ground; for it is time to seek the LORD, until he comes and showers righteousness on you" (Hos. 10:12 NIV).

SUGGESTIONS FOR STABILITY

How can we stay stable in a storm of unexpected circumstances? Here are three more suggestions:

1. Remember that God's sovereign purpose will prevail.

We cannot see the pattern God is weaving into our lives. Only He can take the darkest threads and weave them along with the lighter ones into a beautiful design.

For instance Joseph suffered, but told his brothers, "You intended to harm me, but God intended it for good to accomplish what is now being done, the saving of many lives" (Gen. 50:20 NIV). Joseph looked beyond his trials to see God's bigger plan for his life.

We are comforted in knowing that everything in our lives is Father-filtered. It passes His desk before it ends up in our lives. We can always say with confidence: "Thank You, Lord, I needed that!"

Jacob spells out to his sons the reasons before he pronounces the verdict. Joseph is dead; Simeon is dead (really held hostage) and now you want Benjamin. Verdict: "Everything is against me!"

To Jacob, I would say—a man has no right to an opinion until all the facts are in. God is orchestrating all these circumstances to give you back the full dozen. God is always working behind the scenes on our behalf—even if we cannot see it and cannot understand it. He is sovereign.

2. Stand on His promises in the midst of the storm.

During life's storms we draw upon God's Word to see us through. An excellent reason to maintain a disciplined Bible study is to soak God's truth deeply into the fabric of our lives. The hymn writer says it all:

> Standing on the promises that cannot fail,
> When the howling storms of doubt and fear assail;
> By the Living Word of God I shall prevail,
> Standing on the promises of God.[4]

Paul tells the Romans: "But in all these things we overwhelmingly conquer through Him who loved us" (Rom. 8:37). When my dad was dying of cancer a few years ago, I longed to touch his heart with the Word of God. After the Lord led me to this passage, I found a framed calligraphy of these verses which I bought and gave to him as a gift. The next time I visited him, I was pleased to see it on his wall: "For I am convinced that neither death, nor life, nor angels, nor principalities, nor things present, nor things to come, nor powers, nor height, nor depth, nor any other created thing, shall be able to separate us from the love of God, which is in Christ Jesus our Lord" (Rom. 8:38–39).

3. Remain Steadfast in Service.

Paul's advice is beautifully written—"Be anxious for nothing, but in everything by prayer and supplication with thanksgiving let your requests be made known to God. And the peace of God which surpasses all comprehension, shall guard your hearts and your minds in Christ Jesus" (Phil. 4:6–7).

Peter says essentially the same thing—"Casting all your anxiety upon Him, because He cares for you (1 Pet. 5:7). The psalmist agrees, "We wait in hope for the LORD; he is our help and our shield" (Ps. 33:20 NIV).

A common misconception is that Christians should be exempt from heartaches and tragedy. But this false expectation sets us up for disillusionment, disappointment, and depression—all of which may thwart our wholehearted service.

Trials will come, but instead of being hindered by false expectations, we can be strengthened by trusting Christ in the storm. When this occurs, Scripture is not limited to the printed page. Its powerful truth is integrated into our thoughts, our speech, and our responses. We feel the Holy Spirit's embrace of comfort and the presence of a loving Heavenly Father moved with compassion as he draws us closer.

The Christian need not panic at the unexpected, but see it as an opportunity to stand firm. Our decision to do so honors the Lord. The more we know Him, the more confidently we serve Him.

CHAPTER FOURTEEN

Abiding in the Vine

I am the vine, you are the branches; he who abides in Me and I in him, he bears much fruit; for apart from Me you can do nothing.

JOHN 15:5

One day in Dallas after I'd finished teaching a luncheon class, a businessman with a pained expression on his face, made his way to the front. Fred said, "Don, I have everything I've ever wanted, but with all these possessions I have no time to enjoy them." He seemed frustrated as he added, "You have such joy and peace, what is it with you? I am so stressed, stubborn, and just plain stupid I guess. You'd think with all this success, I'd be satisfied. But that's not the way it is for me. I have no peace, joy, or real sense of fulfillment."

I had just shared that the secret of joyful living is bearing fruit in the lives of others. The secret of bearing fruit is abiding in Christ, and the secret of abiding in Christ is obeying. So I put my hand on Fred's shoulder and said, "Fred, you've got to let Him have it."

He asked, "What do you mean?"

"Give God your will!"

He looked at me with rapt attention as I explained, "Fred, the secret to obeying is loving. You've got to give God your heart. The secret of loving is knowing. You've got to give God your mind. As you surrender your will, your heart, and your mind, God will work, and He will begin bearing fruit in you and through you."

As believers we seek to learn more about this from Christ.

THE TRUE VINE

Why did Jesus teach the disciples about fruit bearing prior to His crucifixion? Could it be that drinking the fruit of the vine brought it to His attention? Maybe His thoughts were triggered by seeing the large vineyard in the Kidron Valley near the Garden of Gethsemene. Or perhaps He noticed a vine inscribed on the door of the temple.

Many Old Testament verses refer to Israel as the vine whom God Himself tended. In obedience the vine flourished, but when Israel rebelled against the Lord, the fruit was missing. So He dealt with it severely.

Then in the New Testament we see Jesus describing Himself as the true vine and God, the Father, as the vinedresser. Jesus was preparing His disciples to understand that when He was no longer visible, the person of the Holy Spirit would indwell believers as their divine enabler. "By this we know that we abide in Him and He in us, because He has given us of His Spirit" (1 John 4:13). In other words, Jesus indwells the believer's heart through the Holy Spirit. How can this be?

C. S. Lovett points out in *Lights for Laymen* that "Television unveils the mystery of Christ's indwelling. Consider how a man in a TV studio brings his presence to an audience. A studio transmitter sends his image to the surrounding area. By means of the carrier waves, he can enter every home with a TV set.

"Jesus in heaven's studio can reproduce His presence by way of the Holy Spirit in every heart which will tune Him in. In a body, He could indwell no one. You can't stuff one body inside another, but in the Spirit, He can enter every heart which will tune in Jesus. If men can infinitely reproduce their presence in homes by means of circuits and transmitters, surely Jesus, by means of His Spirit can infinitely reproduce His presence in hearts."[1]

When we come to know Jesus Christ as Savior, the Spirit of God comes to indwell us permanently. Jesus is telling the disciples, as the curtain is coming down on His earthly ministry, not to worry. I believe He is reassuring the disciples in John 14:26 they will not be left alone. "But the Helper, the Holy Spirit, whom the Father will send in My name, He will teach you all things, and bring to your remembrance all that I said to you."

The Holy Spirit is going to be doing two things for us, according to Jesus.

1. He will be teaching us all things. He is our resident professor tutoring us along the path of obedience.

2. He will recall to our mind all that He said to us. We have the capacity for instant recall with the presence of the Holy Spirit. What joy comes to our heart when the Holy Spirit brings to our mind the very verse or verses that apply to a given situation.

Jesus is the vine and we are the branches. Branches do not have life in themselves. The branch's life is in the vine.

Bill Bright, in his book *Revolution Now,* says, "We do not produce apart from Christ's strength any more than the branch produces fruit apart from the vine. It is the life-giving sap that flows up from the roots through the vine, the overflow of the vine's life, that produces the fruit. So it is in the life of the believer. It is the Holy Spirit working through the vine, which is Jesus

Christ, overflowing into the branches, the Christians, producing the fruit."[2]

So the vine and the branch must be in life-giving union before fruit is produced. The branch doesn't have to strain to produce fruit, it is a natural outgrowth of being in the vine.

In *The Life and Diary of David Brainerd* we read: "I never saw the work of God appear so independent of means as at this time. I discoursed to the people, and spake what I suppose had a proper tendency to promote convictions; for God's manner of working upon them seemed so entirely supernatural, and above means, that I could scarcely believe He used me as an instrument, or what I spoke as means of carrying on His work. It seemed as I thought to have no connection with nor dependence upon means in any respect. Although I could not but continue to use the means which I thought proper for the promotion of the work. Yet, God seemed as I apprehended to work entirely without them. I seemed to do nothing, and indeed to have nothing to do, but to 'stand still and see the salvation of God,' and found myself obliged and delighted to say, 'Not unto us,' not unto instruments and means, 'but to thy name glory.' God appeared to work entirely alone, and I saw no room to attribute any part of this work to any created arm."[3]

WHAT KIND OF FRUIT?

The farmer knows that if he plants peach trees and takes care of them according to their needs, he will reap a crop of peaches. He doesn't expect plums from peach trees or vice versa.

Likewise, if a person abides in Christ, he will produce eternal fruit. Jesus is the vine and the Father is the gardener. He will create any kind of climate he can for maximum productivity which may mean tilling, stirring up the soil, and pruning the branches.

But prior to fruitfulness, submission is required. Just as we surrendered to Christ at the time of conversion, we need the same attitude in regard to bringing forth fruit. We depend upon Christ within us through His Holy Spirit.

Failure on our part to be responsive to His Hand at work in our lives leads to a withered fruitless branch. When Peter would not let Jesus wash his feet, the Lord said: "If I do not wash you, you have no part with Me" (John 13:8). We can quench the life-giving flow of the Spirit in our lives by our resistance.

On the other hand, fruitfulness is the manifestation of Christlike character. "But the fruit of the Spirit is love, joy, peace, patience, kindness, goodness, faithfulness, gentleness, self-control; against such things there is no law" (Gal. 5:22–23).

Examples of some different kinds of fruit God wants to bear in our lives include:

- Witnessing and Soul Winning
- Holiness of Life
- Character
- Sharing Good Works
- Praise and Testimony

I know it sounds incredible but it is nevertheless true, God will work in you and through you to bear fruit that is pleasing to Him. The fruit of this union will be internal and external. First in your life and then in the lives of others.

Stephen Olford points out in his book *I'll Take the High Road*: "God pleases to operate when we stand with eyes clear to see His vision, ears clear to hear His voice, and hearts clear to know His victory."[4]

The hymnwriter Mary Maxwell says it so well:

How I praise Thee, precious Saviour,
That Thy love laid hold of me;

Thou hast saved and cleansed and filled me
That I might Thy channel be.

Emptied that Thou shouldest fill me,
A clean vessel in Thy hand;
With no pow'r but as Thou givest
Graciously with each command.

Witnessing Thy pow'r to save me,
Setting free from self and sin;
Thou who boughtest to possess me,
In Thy fullness, Lord come in.

Jesus, fill now with Thy Spirit
Hearts that full surrender know;
That the streams of living water
From our inner man may flow.

Channels only, blessed Master,
But with all Thy wondrous pow'r
Flowing thro' us, Thou canst use us
Ev'ry day and ev'ry hour.[5]

Whenever I think of Christmas, the word *availability* springs into my thoughts: Jesus, Joseph, and Mary were available for God the Father to use them. When the Angel Gabriel made his call to Mary, her response was: "Behold, the bondslave of the Lord; be it done to me according to your word" (Luke 1:38).

The Christ child was literally formed within her. Paul parallels the spiritual process which occurs within us as he addresses the Galatians: "My children, with whom I am again in labor until Christ is formed in you" (Gal. 4:19). Just as Mary experienced the pain of Jesus' physical birth, Paul anguished over the spiritual growth of those under his leadership. Likewise, as Mary submitted and became a willing servant, our availability is God's opportunity.

HOW DO WE LET GOD ABIDE IN OUR LIVES?

Phillip Keller, in his book *A Gardener Looks at the Fruits of the Spirit*, speaks of "three words that spell out growth in godliness":

1. Acknowledge. Oh, God, You are very God. You know exactly what You are doing with me. It is for my best. All is well.

2. Accept His management. Herein lies peace and rest. No longer will I resist or resent Your work in my life. You are the good gardener.

3. Approve of Christ's arrangement of your affairs. It is God's intention that I should become fruitful. Under His good hand this will happen. I will thank Him for everything. This will turn pouting into praise, grumbling into gratitude. It is the key to releasing all the energies of God, the Holy Spirit, to move fully and freely through my daily life. He will do exceedingly more than I can ever ask or think."[6]

Fruit is nothing more than the result of God working in our lives. The fruit of the womb in the marriage relationship as a result of the union is a precious child. Out of our union with Christ, fruit will be borne. My interpretation of John 15:8 is that fruit bearing is a continuing process. "In this my Father is glorified, that you are bearing much fruit."

The other morning in my devotional time while reading Luke 13:6–9, I began to realize what a priority bearing fruit really is to our Heavenly Father: "And He began telling this parable: 'A certain man had a fig tree which had been planted in his vineyard; and he came looking for fruit on it, and did not find any. And he said to the vineyard-keeper, "Behold, for three years I have come looking for fruit on this fig tree without finding any. Cut it down! Why does it even use up the ground?" And he answered and said to him, "Let it alone, sir, for this year too, until I dig around it and put in fertilizer; and if it bears fruit next year, fine; but if not, cut it down.'"

I found myself praying: "Father, search me, try me, do whatever it takes. I want to be fruitful for You!"

WHAT ABOUT PRUNING?

Just as a farmer or gardener prunes trees for better growth and production, our vinedresser, our Heavenly Father will do what is needed to help us bear fruit. Sometimes the abundant life includes aerating the soil around the roots, pruning, fertilizing, watering—whatever is necessary for greater fruit production. The other day one of my friends said, "The Father sure is nipping at my branch lately."

Many of us can identify with his feelings.

If we are abiding in Christ, we can expect the pruning process as a part of the Father's plan for a bumper crop. Every branch not bearing fruit He is lifting up or He is taking away and every branch that is bearing fruit He is tending. The Father's attitude about both branches is to obtain fruit. Thus He is allowing *stuff* to come into our lives to make us fruitful.

Sometimes we are dealing with bad things and sometimes we allow the good things to distract us from God's perfect will. Then we also have to deal with the little foxes that spoil our vineyard. "Catch for us the foxes, the little foxes that ruin the vineyards, our vineyards that are in bloom" (Song of Sol. 2:15 NIV).

Perhaps the fox is unconfessed sin. We should never feed a little fox—he will grow up and devour us. Maybe the little fox is laziness or carelessness. A little slumber, a little sleep, the little foxes ruin the vineyard. The Christian who becomes lax in spending time alone with God opens the door to temptation in many areas of life.

FRUIT INSPECTION

Annie Johnson Flint in *The Pruned Branch* writes: "It is the branch that bears the fruit that feels the knife, to prune it for a larger growth and fuller life."[7]

When the gardener comes to look at our branch, we may be uneasy. What happens if our branch looks unhealthy? What happens if Jesus sees no fruit?

The branch becomes unfruitful when one of two things has happened: First, the Holy Spirit is grieved by sin or disobedience, or secondly, the Holy Spirit is quenched by our unwillingness to surrender and be submissive to Him.

God will do whatever is necessary to restore the branch to a position of fruitfulness. He may very well introduce us to His three steps to recovery:

1. **Circumstances**—Stirring up the circumstances around us to get a proper response.

2. **Chastening—or Woodshed 101**—It hurts when God disciplines us. Chastening from the hand of our loving Father is an attempt to get us to respond. "All discipline for the moment seems not to be joyful, but sorrowful; yet to those who have been trained by it, afterwards it yields the peaceful fruit of righteousness" (Heb. 12:11).

3. **Conservation—or Come on Home**—in physical death. This is where Christ blows the whistle and pulls us out of the game. Are we as concerned about Christ producing fruit through us as He is about seeing fruit in us? God wants us to produce fruit *before* we go to glory.

ABIDING THROUGH SUFFERING

Even when the child of God feels deserted, obedience and trust are the keys to abiding. The Old Testament prophet, Habakkuk, throws everything on the line as he says, "Though the fig tree does not bud and there are no grapes on the vines, though the olive crop fails and the fields produce no food, though there are no sheep in the pen and no cattle in the stalls, yet I will rejoice in the Lord, I will be joyful in God my Savior" (Hab. 3:17–18 NIV).

Habakkuk is saying, "God, I know You. I trust You. I'm hanging in there with You even when the frost nips the buds on all my fruit trees and the vines have lots of leaves and no grapes. Even when drought kills the corn, weeds choke the wheat, and bugs kill the garden, I'm with You. Even when the mortgage is due, the bank account is dry, my son drops out of college, and my cholesterol and triglyceride levels are dangerously high, I'm on Your team." You never really understand that He is all you need until He is all you have.

HOW DO YOU KNOW IF YOU ARE ABIDING IN HIM?

Three things characterize the abiding life:

1. We are *Drawing* upon all that He is.
2. We are *Depending* upon all that He can do.
3. We are *Developing* into His image.

We are to be abiding in Him and that is active. It is our responsibility to have fellowship with Him, to trust Him, and to have confidence in His ability. We are to let Him abide in us. That is passive. Both relationships are essential, not opposing one another, but operating together in the Christian life.

WHAT DOES "MUCH FRUIT" MEAN?

When I see the term "much fruit" I see it as:

1. *Christlike Character*—what you are as a result of what Christ has done in your life (Gal. 5:22–23).

2. *Confession of Praise*—the fruit of a relationship—expressed in songs and words of praise (Heb. 13:15)

3. *Contributions*—fruit to your account; to make provision for the Lord's work (Phil 4:17–18; 2 Cor. 9:6)

4. *Conduct*—bearing fruit that spreads around the world (Col. 1:6)

5. *Conversions*—people who come to know Christ through you (1 Thess. 2:19–20).

Only you know if you are expressing praise, if you are Christlike and real, and if you are giving with a pure motive.

POINTS TO REMEMBER ABOUT ABIDING

- The Father's function is to create a climate for maximum productivity.
- The Father's hand is never closer to His child than when He is pruning him.
- The branch has one purpose and that is to bear fruit.
- The Father is glorified when we are bearing much fruit.
- Love, joy, and obedience are the evidences of abiding life.
- Christ's joy is independent of external circumstances.
- To be abiding in Christ means to turn everything over to Him, to trust Him, and to thank Him for what He is doing.

A few years out of seminary I was touched by Jesus' words: "Truly, truly, I say to you, unless a grain of wheat falls into the earth and dies, it remains by itself alone; but if it dies, it bears much fruit. He who loves his life loses it, and he who hates his life in this world shall keep it to life eternal" (John 12:24–25). With Jim Elliot's words ringing in my ears: "He is no fool who gives what he cannot keep to gain what he cannot lose."[8] I surrendered afresh to my Father's plan for service. I remember we were singing:

So send I you to labor unrewarded,
To serve unpaid, unloved, unsought, unknown,
To bear rebuke, to suffer scorn and scoffing;
So send I you to toil for Me alone.

So send I you to bind the bruised and broken,
O'er wand'ring souls to work, to weep, to wake,
To bear the burdens of a world aweary;
So send I you to suffer for My sake.

So send I you to loneliness and longing,
With heart a hung'ring for the loved and known,
Forsaking home and kindred, friend and dear one;
So send I you to know My love alone.

So send I you to leave your life's ambition,
To die to dear desire, self-will resign,
To labor long and love where men revile you;
So send I you to lose your life in Mine.

So send I you to hearts made hard by hatred,
To eyes made blind because they will not see,
To spend, tho' it be blood to spend and spare not;
So send I you to taste of Calvary.

As the Father hath sent me,
So send I you.[9]

CHAPTER FIFTEEN

Harvesting for Him

...I say to you, lift up your eyes, and look on the fields, that they are white for harvest.

JOHN 4:35

As John Baird, third generation Wyoming rancher put it, "You can't ranch cows sittin' in the bunkhouse, drinkin' coffee and readin' books about cows!"[1] Neither can we be effective in reaching others for Christ by just talking about it. We can begin by planting seeds. But how?

Any nugget of truth from God's Word can start an unbeliever thinking. The Holy Spirit can take a question or a thought and use it to bring conviction in a person's heart.

One good reason for us to be involved in Bible study is so we can relate ordinary subjects to scriptural truths. Some evangelistic situations in the Bible began with a casual conversation. For instance, when Philip approached the Ethiopian eunuch and noticed him sitting in his chariot reading the prophet Isaiah, he asked a simple question: "Do you understand what you are reading?"

The eunuch indicated he needed help and invited Philip to

join him, so Philip climbed up into the chariot and began sharing Jesus. As they rode along, the eunuch spotted some water along the road, and he asked to be baptized. They stopped and jumped from the chariot. Philip baptized him. The Holy Spirit then led Philip in another direction, but the eunuch went on his way rejoicing (see Acts 8:26–40).

Farmers know that after sowing seed, it will take months to reap the harvest. This occurs in spiritual matters as well—"One sows, and another reaps" (John 4:37). Paul tells the Corinthians: "I planted, Apollos watered, but God was causing the growth" (1 Cor. 3:6). But sometimes as with the eunuch, the harvest of a soul may occur immediately after the sowing. This was also the case in the outcast Samaritan woman at the well (see John 4:7–30).

Jesus and the disciples had been walking a long distance. They were tired, hot, and hungry. While the disciples went into the city to buy food at the Samaritan Safeway, Jesus sat by the well.

While He was sitting there, a Samaritan woman came to draw water and Jesus spoke to her saying, "Give Me a drink." She was shocked because Jews avoided the Samaritans. They would never drink out of the same dipper, and a Jewish rabbi would never speak to a woman in public, especially a Samaritan woman.

Then Jesus told her the difference between physical water which is temporary and spiritual water which is eternal. He knew all about her past, that she had five husbands and the man she was currently living with was not her husband. She thought Jesus was a prophet. But she also knew the Messiah would be coming.

Then Jesus said, "I who speak to you am He."

She believed Him and she accepted His gift, the living water of eternal life. She left her water pot, went into the city, and told the men about meeting Jesus. "He gave me a computer printout on my life. Do you think He might be the Messiah?" Her powerful testimony caused the people to check it out. They began flocking to the Lord because they witnessed the change in her. She had met the Savior and knew immediately that He had the answers she needed. You can almost hear her singing: "What a wonderful change in my life has been wrought since Jesus came into my heart…"

At other times, months or even years may elapse before a decision is made. Such was the case with Rick Jackson, a faithful student in one of my home Bible study classes in Broken Arrow, Oklahoma.

Rick recently described his salvation experience in a taped interview:

> When my boss and his wife, Junior and Joan, invited my wife, Michele, and me to their home for the Don Anderson Bible study, I was glad they invited us, but I didn't have any background. As a young person, my family went to church on Christmas and Easter, but I wasn't involved. It wasn't important to me. I thought I could start going to church later on when I got older and had a family.
>
> Michele might have been considered a Jesus Freak in her college days but she had kind of slipped away. Then in 1989 she rededicated her life to the Lord and was baptized. Afterwards, she put just the right amount of pressure on me. After sixteen years, Michele knows me pretty well. She planted the seed and nourished it and it started to grow. We talked about it several times and I knew I needed to do something.
>
> After attending Don's Bible studies for about two years, Michele and I went to a couples' conference at Kaleo Lodge. We were sitting on the screened-in porch

deck one morning when Don came by and asked, "Do you have a second to talk with me?"

I said, "Yes."

We went into his office and Don said, "Rick, have you ever asked the Lord into your heart?

I said, "No. I know the Lord's there knocking, but I've never opened the door."

Don said, "Do you want to now?"

I said, "Yes."

Don helped me pray the sinner's prayer and it has changed my life, especially at work. I work at a roofing company and we have quite a bit of pressure there. I used to be impatient and want everything done right now. But since meeting the Lord, my temperament has mellowed and I don't get fired up as much as I used to. I just say, "Next time we'll try to do better."

The people I work with are not all Christians so I try to witness without turning them off. I say what I can and then back off and try again.

It's exciting for me to know Jesus because I used to be afraid of death, but I'm not anymore. When the pastor of my church recently started talking about the end times, I wanted to know more about it. That topic used to scare the daylights out of me, but now I'm not scared anymore.

My relationship with Christ is important. He is a friend to me and I try to be a good friend to Him. I'm studying the Word and going to church, but I feel like I've got a lot of catching up to do. But one thing I do know. It's never too late to ask Jesus into your life.

When I asked Don to baptize me, he came to Tulsa and on August 4, 1995, he baptized me in Junior and Joan's swimming pool.

SOWING AND REAPING

It is only fair to point out that Rick had been watching the lives of people who knew the Lord, and he saw a difference. They had been faithfully planting and sowing. Observing the Christian walk of his wife, as well as his boss and his boss's wife had already helped prepare Rick's heart before harvest time. So at Kaleo Lodge when I posed the question, he was ready. I just reaped the harvest that had already been sown.

Often we see one person sowing—sometimes for a long time—with much prayer and anguish. Then another comes in to reap the harvest of a changed life through conversion. But whether we are sowing or reaping, we are being obedient, and we leave the results in God's hands.

John G. Mitchell writes, "William Carey of India said, 'My job as a missionary is to tell people about the Savior. I just cobble shoes to pay the way.' I don't know what your job is. That's not important. Maybe God gave you that job to help pay the way for yourself or others to share the gospel. But your primary job, from the moment you accepted the Savior is be available for Him to use you in the lives of others."[2]

In 2 Peter 3:9, Peter expresses it beautifully: "The Lord is not slow about His promise, as some count slowness, but is patient toward you, not wishing any to perish but for all to come to repentance."

Jesus expressed His deep concerns: "And seeing the multitudes, He felt compassion for them, because they were distressed and downcast like sheep without a shepherd. Then He said to His disciples, 'The harvest is plentiful, but the workers are few. Therefore beseech the Lord of the harvest to send out workers into His harvest'" (Matt. 9:36–38).

The Lord reached out to all levels of society and He is our example. He extended himself to Nicodemus, Zaccheus,

Matthew, Peter, James, and John. He even reached out to Judas Iscariot. Rich or poor, famous or unknown, friend or foe, Jesus excluded no one. Nor should we.

Is He calling you to get involved in the lives of people who need you? What is your response? Are you willing to respond with the words of Isaiah: "Here am I, send me"? If so, God will use you.

PERSEVERANCE

Rick's testimony is a good example of fruit born through perseverance. It reminds me of Psalm 126:5–6: "Those who sow in tears will reap with songs of joy. He who goes out weeping, carrying seed to sow, will return with songs of joy, carrying sheaves with him" (NIV).

The focus is on staying with it, hanging in there. How many wives have seen their husbands come to Christ because of prayer, perseverance, and consistent witness? Perseverance is part of the process that leads to life eternal.

Bill Hull pushes my button when he says: "Much of contemporary spirituality is trying to have a microwave harvest. The proponents advocate the *greenhouse* approach. Like agrarian scientists, they use the latest tools, technology, and techniques to create a quicker and larger harvest. But in the end nothing can be successful and sustained unless it submits to the basic physical laws of the farm."[3]

God is the One who encourages us to persevere and continue in His plans. His promise is especially meaningful to me as I am getting older. "They will still bear fruit in old age, they will stay fresh and green" (Ps. 92:14 NIV).

Sometimes we may be confused about the difference between patience and perseverance. Both concepts are used in Colossians 1:11, "Strengthened with all power, according to His glorious might, for the attaining of all steadfastness and patience."

Both patience and perseverance are qualities of a godly person, but the words do not have the same meaning.

Patience	**Perseverance**
Passive	Active
Sees the sovereignty of God	Sees God through suffering
Focuses on the plan of God	Focuses on the purposes of God
Magnifies submission	Magnifies the struggle
Focuses on the process	Focuses on the pain
Is a virtue	Leads to victory
Is reactive	Is proactive
Is an attitude	Is an action

Jesus is the model of perseverance. He said, "We must work the works of Him who sent Me, as long as it is day; night is coming, when no man can work" (John 9:4).

Paul is a classic illustration of perseverance. "For this reason I endure all things for the sake of those who are chosen, that they also may obtain the salvation which is in Christ Jesus and with it eternal glory" (2 Tim. 2:10). Paul doesn't see any room for retirement or for letting up, just because one is getting older.

Perseverance is a part of the plan, a character trait of the godly which develops from self-control. Dwight L. Moody once said, "I get weary in the work, but not weary of the work."[4]

After having their fifth child, a couple received a playpen from some friends. Several weeks later the friends who sent the gift received this lighthearted note of thanks: "The playpen is wonderful. Just what we needed. I sit in it every afternoon and read, and the kids can't even get close to me." I call that creative perseverance!

It is obvious from many New Testament passages that perseverance brings pleasure to the Lord Jesus. Steadfastness reveals the depth of Christian commitment and the level of faithfulness. Both pain and endurance are in the plan of God. We are to be laboring until He comes.

Steven Lawson writes in *Men Who Win*, "I fear there are too many 'one-hundred-yard-dash' Christians. They begin well, sprinting out of the starting blocks. They are at the church every time the door is opened. They read their Bibles and their enthusiasm is obvious to all. But eventually, they burn out and drop by the wayside. They go up like a rocket. And come down like a rock. In the day-to-day grind of the race, they eventually weaken, waver, and lose heart."[5]

Someone asked me after discovering I had participated in several marathons, "Did you ever run 26.3 miles all at one time without stopping?"

My answer was, "No, I always ran as far as I could and then walked a little and ran some more. Finishing was the most important thing. Whether I ran or walked, the main thing was to finish."

I have figured out that in any situation it is always right to persevere. We become recipients of God's grace while persisting. We experience growth. God gets the glory.

Nothing thrills your heart any more than seeing your own children hanging in there when it would have been so easy to throw in the towel and quit. Becky was diagnosed with diabetes at age thirteen. She went through the stages that brought her to kidney failure and dialysis. A young man in his late teens living in Florida had the foresight to sign a donor card. He lost his life in a motorcycle accident, but in the process gave life to our Becky in the gift of a kidney. God had another wonderful gift for our sweetheart in leading her to her husband, Ray. She wrote me this letter that says it all:

> Dear Dad,
>
> I remember the Christmas I gave you the plaque you now keep on your desk that says, "It is well with my

soul." Well, as time goes on I realize how much more important for it to be well with my soul than for it to be well with my physical body.

I recall when I was on dialysis and my eyesight was getting worse. I expressed my fears of being blind to Ray and I'll never forget his words: "Honey, I know that would be hard on you, but all it would mean to me is that I'd get to walk a little closer to you." This not only reminds me of God's unconditional love, but it also reminds me of the way suffering lets us "walk a little closer" to God.

When I was younger, I prayed often to be healed of my illness. I always got the same answer as Paul—God's grace would be sufficient for me. Now I understand how wonderful God's grace is. God healed me emotionally by doing a miracle and bringing Ray into my life. God has given me more love and joy during my marriage to Ray than most people experience in a lifetime.

When I am tempted to fear death, I remind myself that it is God's love flowing through Ray to me that brings me so much joy in this life and how wonderful it will be when I get to heaven and experience Christ's pure love.

It is seeing God in the lives of others like you, Mom, and Ray, Dad, that strengthens my faith and keeps me strong.

Thanks, Dad.

I love you,
Becky

COMPASSION

In English, the term *compassion* means a "sympathetic consciousness of another's distress together with a desire to alleviate it." The Hebrew word for compassion means "to be soft." A person can easily be moved emotionally and can be so affected as to respond to the distress of another with tender, gentle, soothing sympathy.

What is the difference between love and compassion? Love is a matter of the heart and compassion is a matter of the hand. Love motivates me and sympathy moves me. "Little children, let us not love with word or with tongue, but in deed and truth" (1 John 3:18).

Compassion is certainly an important element in reaching others for Christ. Our Lord is the epitome of empathy. Throughout His ministry He acknowledges this and told the disciples He felt compassion for the multitudes.

Jesus urges us to go where people have needs and to get involved. To further explain, He tells a story that has the elements of a first rate Clint Eastwood flick: the good, the bad, and the ugly. The good guys include a man going to Jericho and a Samaritan. The bad guys are the robbers. The ugly guys are a priest and a Levite.

A traveling man has been robbed, beaten, and left half-dead in the road. He is battered, bloodied, and helpless. This poor man in Jesus' parable in Luke 10:30–37 represents our mission field. He is a picture of our world. Every day we encounter the depressed, divorced, destroyed, and the devastated. People whose castles have crumbled, visions have vanished, and dreams have been destroyed. Who will reach out and help them?

In Jesus' story, a priest spots the wounded traveler but passes by on the opposite side. His DayTimer is filled, his schedule packed. He is overcommitted, a real workaholic who has become hardened to the needs of others. He doesn't have time to deal with the inconvenience of a hurting, helpless person.

Another person, a Levite, comes along and also avoids the traveler by passing on the other side. The two religious characters in Jesus' story refuse to get involved. Jesus tells us to love one another. It's easy to talk about love, but to really love means to accept certain obligations.

In regard to this passage, Charles H. Spurgeon points out that the priest and the Levite "were very familiar with things which should have softened their hearts...as near to God as man could be, [the priest] serving amidst sacrifices and holy psalms and solemn prayers, and yet he had not learned how to make a sacrifice of himself...yet he came away with a hard heart. This is a sad fact. They had been near to God, but were not like Him."[6]

Unfortunately, these religious men believed that service is in the sanctuary and not in the street. Passing out hymnals, setting up chairs, taking the offering—to them these constituted service. Others could deal with beaten, broken men. They preferred the comfortable cloister to the cry of the crowd. Studies and sofas don't constitute service.

Could it be that we, too, make excuses—perhaps like these:

I'm too tired; I could get sued; I've already done my church duties; I don't know CPR; I have too many appointments; Mama has supper waiting.

After the religious men pass by, another man comes on the scene, a Samaritan who has compassion. This compassion motivates him to approach the bloody traveler, bandage his wounds, and pour on oil and wine, the medicinal treatments of his day. Instead of leaving him beside the road, he places him on his beast, leads him to an inn, and takes care of him.

The next morning the Samaritan pays the innkeeper and gives him these instructions regarding the man, "Take care of him; and whatever more you spend, when I return, I will repay you" (Luke 10:35). Think of what the Samaritan does: He alters his schedule, administers first-aid, walks so the wounded man can ride to the inn, and he pays for the stranger's convalescence.

If we had been victimized, who would we wish to come by? The priest, the Levite, or the Samaritan? Genuine compassion moves us to action. It is more than a warm, fuzzy feeling. It is more than pity. It is love in action. May God help us if we are becoming men and women who are cold, compassionless cowards when it comes to the matter of being involved in the lives of others.

Someone has wisely said: Fundamentalism is an excuse for being uninvolved. Orthodoxy without opportunity is obnoxious. Theology without a theater is terrible. Doctrine without a demonstration is dead. Instruction must result in involvement or it will become invalid.

AVAILABILITY

What God wants is our availability. We don't have to be preachers or teachers to share the gospel of Christ. The Lord just wants us to be sensitive to those around us. If we're walking closely with Him, we'll hear His voice and know when He is prompting us to give a word of testimony, hand out a tract, share hospitality, or ask a pertinent question.

In short, God wants us to be concerned about the souls of those around us. The person who sows is just as important as the one who reaps. They are equal in God's sight. When we are available, God is ready to use us.

Jon Mohr wrote a verse whose words speak of the necessity of making our lives a "sacrament of the present moment:"

> Oh may all who come behind us find us faithful
> May the fires of our devotion light the way
> May the footprints that we leave
> Lead them to believe
> And the lives we lead inspire them to obey.[7]

Conclusion

CHAPTER SIXTEEN

Celebrating with Joy!

Rejoice in the Lord always; again I will say, rejoice!

PHILIPPIANS 4:4

My friend, Ron Bower, along with Robert White and Kirk Hays, formed a company in Austin, Texas, called Austin Jet. Many times through the years when commercial flight schedules haven't met my needs, Robert, Ron, and Kirk have volunteered pilots and planes to shuttle me from place to place to teach my classes. Only eternity will reveal all these guys have done to make my ministry possible.

Ron's passion is helicopters, and he handles that part of the business. For a long time, Ron had a desire to break the speed record for a solo helicopter flight around the world. To do so he set out to cross 23,591 miles, 21 countries, and 24 time zones in 24 days. Ron achieved his goal on July 22, 1994, beating the previous record by almost five days.

Dressed in an orange jumpsuit, black boots, and a cap with a world-map insignia, Ron hopped out of his aircraft soon after touching down near Fort Worth. He kissed both the ground and his helicopter before exclaiming, "It's good to be home!" Then the celebration with family and friends began.

Most of us view such occasions shaking our heads and saying, "I can't believe he did that!" We extol high achievers because their names are in the record books. They've distinguished themselves from the rest of us in their area of expertise.

Christians rejoice because we know Christ. He gives us life abundantly. Just as military leaders acclaim war victories, athletes revel in feats of courage, and farmers applaud successful harvests, we rejoice in knowing He will strengthen us for our task, whatever He has called us to do.

"For I am confident of this very thing, that He who began a good work in you will perfect it until the day of Christ Jesus" (Phil. 1:6). He will continue to work in our lives until we go to be with Him in our heavenly home. But until then, how can we sustain our joy?

OUR SOURCE OF JOY

Joy is the flag that flies when the King is in residence, occupying the throne of our hearts. The joy of the Lord is the result of a relationship with Him and does not depend upon the circumstances in our lives. "You will fill me with joy in your presence" (Ps. 16:11 NIV).

JOY IS MANIFESTED IN FOUR AREAS OF THE CHRISTIAN'S LIFE

1. Joy is the evidence of salvation.

When we realize our sins are forgiven, exhilarating joy enters in. We are free from bondage. Even heaven rejoices when one sinner repents (Luke 15:7).

If sin is not dealt with or if it is excused, we feel guilty. At the same time, we are permitting the damaging consequences of sin to separate us from fellowship with the Father. After David's sin with Bathsheba and Nathan's confrontation, David acknowledged his personal responsibility for sin and his lack of joy. He prayed a sinner's prayer for pardon pleading, "Restore to me the joy of your salvation" (Ps. 51:12 NIV).

2. Joy is the evidence of fellowship.

Joy is the evidence of fellowship with the Lord. "...what we have seen and heard we proclaim to you also, that you may have fellowship with us; and indeed our fellowship is with the Father, and with His Son, Jesus Christ. And these things we write, so that our joy may be made complete" (1 John 1:3–4).

Fellowship is enhanced through comradeship, sharing common interests, and spending time together. Those who experience a close walk with the Lord are comfortable talking with Him in prayer or mentioning Him in conversation. It seems only natural because of our love for Him. However, if we lose that close association with the Lord, joy is the first thing to go.

If this happens we need to examine ourselves. Are we harboring unconfessed sin? If so, we hesitate to mention His name, and we often fail to spend time with Him. Lonely and unhappy believers need to ask themselves: Is something missing? The formula is:

Abiding
\+ the Word working in my life
\+ Fruit
= JOY

When we're in fellowship with our Lord, He uses us in the lives of others and joy results.

3. Joy is the evidence of a right response to trial.

Trials will come into our lives as believers, and joy is the response of expectation.

"And not only this, but we also exult in our tribulations; knowing that tribulation brings about perseverance; and perseverance, proven character; and proven character, hope" (Rom. 5:3–4).

One of the hallmarks of the New Testament church was joy in the midst of persecution. For the early Christians and for us, joy does not depend upon our circumstances. It is a fruit of the spirit and a part of the spirit-filled life. "And the disciples were continually filled with joy and with the Holy Spirit" (Acts 13:52).

As a believer I'll choose not to whine, "God, why did You let this happen?" Rather, I'll search for a deeper meaning and ask expectantly, "Lord, how are You going to use this in my life for good?"

Jesus is our example—"...who for the joy set before Him, endured the cross..." (Heb. 12:2). "These things I have spoken to you, that My joy may be in you, and that your joy may be made full" (John 15:11). How could Jesus have had joy the night before His crucifixion? It was the response of anticipation. He looked beyond the cross and the tomb to see that He would purchase salvation and redemption for all mankind. Likewise, we can look beyond our crisis and know that God can bring beauty from ashes.

One time Pearl and I were having dinner at Luby's and I told her that I'd soon be writing on James 1:2—"Consider it all joy, my brethren, when you encounter various trials."

To which she quickly sighed, "Lord, help us all!"

We never talk about James 1 without a chance to practice it. James says we grow through trials. It's tough, we reject it, but James assures us we'll have joy on the other end of the line.

My good buddy Larry Beal writes:

> God has given Jill and me three kids; the youngest is autistic. God has taught me a valuable lesson through her.

> One night as I was praying for her, I was pouring out my frustration to God about how I wanted to communicate with her. I wanted to somehow break through the veil of autism that had hidden her heart from me. If only she could talk to me, I cried out to God. How will I ever get to know her if I can't talk to her, or her to me? How will she ever understand? She is just wrapped up in her own little world and there is no way to break through.
>
> At the height of my concern for my daughter before God, He answered me and said, 'You Are Autistic to Me.' At that moment I realized how God feels about me. I don't listen; I do things my own way. I don't talk to him. I'm in my own little world. But most of all, I realized how much God is longing for me to communicate with him. God sure chooses unusual ways to teach us.[1]

Even at the time of death, we can be crying at the loss of a loved one and still have joy. The expectancy is that home-going is more wonderful than we ever imagined. God never makes a mistake.

4. Joy is the evidence of a right response to heaven.

"And though you have not seen Him, you love Him, and though you do not see Him now, but believe in Him, you greatly rejoice with joy inexpressible and full of glory" (1 Pet. 1:8). Just think what heaven will be like when we stand before Him, our race finished, and we're in His presence.

On Saturday, April 6, 1991, just forty-eight hours before his departure, my friend and confidant, John MacKinnon wrote these final words:

> "In my Father's house are many mansions" (John 14:2) is the scripture reading from my desk calendar today. Can

you imagine? Mansions within a house. And He has gone there to prepare for me. Not only a mansion, but He is there making it ready. Did you ever have the feeling that your…"[2]

In his weakness, John was not able to complete that sentence. I'm sure if he could have written more, he would have asked, "Did you ever have the feeling that your time has come and that your house is ready?"

JOY THROUGH LIFE'S DIFFERENT PHASES

A surprise brought me joy one morning at our Colorado camp. All week I'd thought about ceremonially retiring my running shoes at 5 A.M. with nobody around. I visualized myself sneaking out for a last run, putting my marathon shoes to bed forever. I knew in my heart that hip replacement surgery, scheduled for the following Tuesday would change my life forever.

When I slipped down the hill to the main highway, I thought I was alone until I saw Doug, Joe, and Tom waiting for me yelling, "Hey, Don! We're going to help you finish!"

They jogged beside me and when we reached the five-mile mark, there stood Sara, smiling and holding a big poster of Philippians 3:14: "I press on toward the goal for the prize of the upward call of God in Christ Jesus."

Just as I crossed the finish line, she clicked on a prerecorded crowd cheering wildly in stereophonic sound. Wow! My friends made me feel great! My final run was completed, with the help of a lot of friends. I've discovered joy in putting things behind me and also joy in finishing what I set out to do. Now I'll go on to something new.

In a similar way, I believe joy will fill our hearts when we cooperate with God's eternal plan to help us become more

Christlike. Thankfully, we have friends who come alongside to encourage us along the way and to whom we can be accountable.

One of the greatest inspirations on earth is an elderly person overflowing with joy. The Spirit-filled man or woman who laughs at their frailties and maintains a sense of humor, in spite of aches and pains, encourages us all. Boy, I want to be like that, too!

LIVING WITH JOY

As Paul writes to the Philippians from prison, we see his incredible ability to rise above his circumstances and to express joy—a good lesson for us to remember when things are tough. Here are nine concepts he proposes to help us maintain joy in daily living.

1. Convictions

"Therefore, my beloved brethren whom I long to see, my joy and crown, so stand firm in the Lord, my beloved" (Phil. 1:1).

First, he urges us to **stand firm**, not to be double-minded and unstable in all our ways and tossed about by every wind of doctrine. But we are to be standing firm in the Lord. Also, we're to put on all of God's armor so we can stand safe against the wiles of Satan.

Three Ps can keep us from standing firm:

Problems—Don't say, "This problem is so great I quit." Don't throw in the towel.

Pressures—Don't say, "The pressure is so great I'll compromise for the sake of peace." Don't cave in.

Persecution—Don't say, "It just isn't worth it to give of myself." Remember Daniel who purposed in his heart to honor God. Don't be afraid. God can handle the lions.

We need men and women who realize that it will cost something to be what God wants us to be and to do what God wants us to do. More of us need to stand firm in our convictions and not let problems, pressures, or persecution hinder us from standing firm.

2. *Concord*

"I urge Euodia and Syntyche to live in harmony in the Lord" (Phil. 4:2).

Paul urges these two ladies to be of one accord in unity and oneness because they've gotten into a fuss. They should be living their convictions, but they're too busy shooting at each other. I call them "Odorous" and "Soon Touchy."

How do we want to be remembered? What sentence would epitomize our lives right now? If we harbor grudges and a contentious spirit, we, too, will be causing problems in the church. The Lord wants us to live in peace and harmony which contributes to our joy.

Unfortunately, we sometimes operate with subtraction and division, but the Spirit wants addition and multiplication. Our unity becomes our witness for Christ. As the little chorus says, "They will know we are Christians by our love."

3. *Compassion*

"Indeed, true comrade, I ask you also to help these women who have shared my struggle in the cause of the gospel, together with Clement also, and the rest of my fellow-workers, whose names are in the book of life" (Phil. 4:3).

Paul is exhorting his good friends to assist these women and to manifest compassion toward them. They are to share each other's troubles and problems and he focuses on one fellow to help as a mediator in getting their differences resolved.

Then he addresses the rest of the people whose names are written in the Book of Life. Recorded on the day of our new birth, our names are written in the Lamb's Book of Life (Rev. 20:15). The absence of a name in the book provides the justice for the eternal judgment and condemnation at the great white throne when unbelievers will be thrown into the lake of fire.

However, multitudes of people whose names have not been published in a newspaper on any occasion except for birth and death announcements, will be recorded in the Lamb's Book of Life because they have placed their faith and trust in the Lord Jesus Christ.

Christ's compassion for us brings joy we can share with others.

One day I had an opportunity to lead Bobby Brown to the Lord. Bobby was a third baseman for the New York Yankees during their golden years. He played with Bobby Richardson who, when he retired, traveled around the country sharing his Christian testimony. On a television show one night, he closed with this poem which I really like:

Your name may not appear down here
In this world's Hall of Fame,
In fact, you may be so unknown
That no one knows your name;
The Oscars and the praise of men
May never come your way,
But don't forget God has rewards
That He'll hand out someday.

This Hall of Fame is only good
As long as time shall be;
But keep in mind, God's Hall of Fame
Is for eternity;

To have your name inscribed up there
Is greater more by far
Than all the fame and all the praise
Of ev'ry man-made star.

This crowd on earth may soon forget
When you're not at the top.
They'll cheer like mad until you fall
And then their praise will stop;
Not God, He never does forget,
And in His Hall of Fame,
By just believing on His Son,
Forever—there's your name.

I tell you, friend, I wouldn't trade
My name, however small,
That's written there beyond the stars
In that celestial Hall;
For all famous names on earth,
Or glory that they share;
I'd rather be an unknown here,
And have my name up there.[3]

4. Circumstances

"Rejoice in the Lord always; again I will say, rejoice!" (Phil. 4:4). Be rejoicing is a double command. Regardless of the difficulties we encounter, we are to be rejoicing in the Lord. When we have joy in traumatic circumstances three things are true.

- We have submitted to it.
- We are seeking wisdom to respond to it.

- We are accepting grace available to triumph in the midst of it.

During trials, Paul has the joy of expectation and the joy of anticipation. Just like Pearl always says in the midst of trials, "This, too, shall pass."

Think of trials like a woman in labor. Afterward, she gives birth to something pretty precious. Likewise, our pain gives birth to something priceless. The joyful keep going and it can only be done "in the Lord."

To triumph in joy in all situations we can be:

1. Awake to His Power
2. Attuned to His Plan
3. Assured of His Presence

5. Character

"Let your forbearing spirit be known to all men. The Lord is near" (Phil. 4:5).

How should we convey our character? What is our sweet reasonableness to be known among all men? It means to be satisfied with less than we deserve. It is the opposite of demanding our rights; it is giving in, being sensitive, gentle, tenderhearted, and kind. Relating to others in this manner brings joy to life. My Pearl is so much like that. She would have to be to survive all these years with me. We are closing in on the gold. Her sweet spirit makes it so easy to talk; her gentleness has made her great.

6. Concerns

"Be anxious for nothing, but in everything by prayer and supplication with thanksgiving let your requests be made known to God" (Phil. 4:6).

Paul is addressing their concerns. He says don't be worried—pray. Mark Twain says, "I am an old man and have known a great many troubles, but most of them never happened."[4] At the bottom of all our worry and concern is unbelief. We don't believe that God is adequate to handle the situation so we have to worry about it. Bill Gothard defines worry as "assuming responsibility God never intended us to have."[5] Haddon Robinson says, "What worries you masters you."[6]

When we get our eyes off the Lord and on our circumstances, we fret and are robbed of joy. Corrie Ten Boom says, "Worry does not empty tomorrow of its sorrow; it empties today of its strength."[7] Instead, we can choose to cast our cares upon Him and pray. Nothing is too great for our Lord to handle. When we fail to pray we limit ourselves to our own resources, but in the midst of our prayers we are freed from anxieties and concerns. Be anxious for nothing, prayerful in everything, and thankful for anything.

7. Composure

His peace and joy become ours as we obey. "And the peace of God, which surpasses all comprehension, shall guard (hold in custody) your hearts and your minds in Christ Jesus" (Phil. 4:7).

A great little devotional book, *Let Go,* by François Fenelon gives some helpful advice:

> Live in continued peace but understand that peace does not depend upon the fervor of your devotion, the only thing you need to be concerned about is the direction of your will.
>
> Learn to cultivate peace and you can do this by learning to turn a deaf ear to your own ambitions and thoughts. Or haven't you yet learned that the strivings of

> the human mind not only impair the health of your body, but also bring dryness to the soul. You can actually consume yourself by too much inner striving and to no purpose at all. Your peace and inner sweetness can be des-troyed by a restless mind.
>
> Satan is the one who torments us with trivialities and he often transforms himself into an angel of light and bothers us with endless self-examinations and an over-sensitive conscience which allows us no peace.[8]

Peace is the quiet, potent, gracious, attitude of serenity and goodwill that comes to meet the onslaught of others with good cheer, equanimity, and strong repose. The peace of God acts as an umpire in our lives (Col. 3:15) and contributes to our joy.

8. Concepts

When we are told to have the mind of Christ according to Philippians 4:8, this is the menu: "Finally, brethren, whatever is true, whatever is honorable, whatever is right, whatever is pure, whatever is lovely, whatever is of good repute, if there is any excellence and if anything worthy of praise, let your mind dwell on these things."

As we think these thoughts, we erect a barrier to Satan. Sometimes it helps to keep this verse handy as a reminder. Living through the strength of Christ is our final goal. Just as commitment, discipline, and pure old hard work are the necessary ingredients for becoming a soldier, an athlete, or a farmer, the same is true for a Christian.

Christ takes us beyond our own human capacity and resources. What a joy to feel His strength indwelling us! Paul longed to experience His resurrection power because he realized his weakness.

As a Bible teacher for thirty-five years, I've been involved in some very difficult situations. Occasionally someone will observe, "I just couldn't go through what that person has." But what they need to understand is that God gives the strength we need to go through His curriculum for our lives. In our weakness, His strength is made perfect.

Paul tells us in 2 Corinthians 12:9: "And He has said to me, 'My grace is sufficient for you, for power is perfected in weakness.' Most gladly, therefore, I will rather boast about my weaknesses, that the power of Christ may dwell in me."

While praying to the Father, I often feel a note of praise welling up in my heart. My heart swells with God's goodness as I say: Thank You for Your power. I see its awesome display in creation. I see it every day in my conversion. I rely upon it in my spiritual conflict. I can hardly wait to see it when You split the skies and call us home. "All hail the power of Jesus' name, let angels prostrate fall! Bring forth the royal diadem, and crown Him Lord of all."

9. Contentment

Contentment comes when we:

Accept ourselves. We are valuable in the Lord's sight. We each have a contribution to make. It isn't wise to compare our gifts with others. We should be using the ones God has given us.

Accept His plan. If we are operating in God's will, we can be content. However, many times we are busily involved in our own plans instead of His. Frustration is usually the result, not joy.

Accept His provision. He will always provide exceedingly abundantly above all that we are willing to think. If we have lack of contentment, we're usually withholding some critical area of our lives from the Lordship of Christ. When we surrender our wills to Him, we will become contented.

Paul tells the Philippian saints this was something he had to learn: "Not that I speak from want; for I have learned to be content in whatever circumstances I am" (Phil. 4:11).

George Bernard Shaw, Irish playwright and agnostic, writes:

> This is the true joy in life, being used for a purpose recognized by yourself as a mighty one.
>
> Being a force of nature instead of a feverish selfish little clod of ailments and grievances complaining that the world will not devote itself to making you happy.
>
> I am of the opinion that my life belongs to the whole community and as long as I live it is my privilege to do for it whatever I can.
>
> I want to be thoroughly used up when I die. For the harder I work the more I live. I rejoice in life for its own sake. Life is no brief candle to me; it's a sort of splendid torch which I've got to hold up for the moment and I want to make it burn as brightly as possible before handing it on to future generations.[9]

I will take issue by saying: "I agree with Paul. My life belongs to the Savior, and as long as I live it is my privilege to do for Him whatever I can."

Let's return to that dark, damp, dungeon where our beloved friend is just now finishing his lines to young Timothy. In the flickering candlelight we read over his shoulder: "For I am already being poured out as a drink offering and the time of my departure is imminent. I have fought a good fight, I have finished the race, I have kept (guarded) the faith..." The clock is ticking. Paul's flight is ready to depart.

Paul, are you sad?

To paraphrase Philippians 2:17–18—"Oh no! I am a weary

traveler and I have finished my Father's business, and I am going home! How could I be sad? I told the Philippians that 'Even if I am being poured out as a drink offering upon the sacrifice and service of your faith, I am joying and rejoicing with you all. But you also, be rejoicing in the same thing and be rejoicing with me."

"I am totally spent and spilled out. I have given myself fully to the Savior and His plan for me. I am so filled with joy. I am ready for some celebrating!"

You know, what Paul says is really true. One of the greatest joys in eternity will be knowing we gave ourselves away in sacrificial involvement. Every day is a joy to live as we learn how to Give! Give! Give!

Lord! When I come home on the flight You've scheduled for me, I hope I can say: "I have fought, I was faithful, and I finished." I am longing to hear You say: "Well done, good and faithful servant."

Study Guide

The following questions may be used for individual study or group discussions.

CHAPTER 1
BEGINNING BASIC TRAINING

1. In your own words explain the meaning of:
   a. Justification

   b. Atonement

2. Is it possible to have peace with God? How?

3. Based upon Scripture, name four benefits of those who receive Christ.

4. What Scripture in this chapter especially spoke to you?

5. Write out the following Scriptures and personalize them:
   Romans 3:23
   Romans 6:23
   Romans 10:9–10
   Ephesians 5:8

6. Has the Holy Spirit prompted you regarding a decision you need to make?

CHAPTER 2
GETTING TO KNOW THE COMMANDER-IN-CHIEF

1. How can we get to know the Commander-in-Chief?

2. What do you learn about Him from the following Scriptures?

Psalm 31:3
Psalm 32:8
Isaiah 28:29
Jeremiah 9:24
1 John 1:5
1 John 2:1–2
1 John 4:7–8

3. What is the difference between reading and studying God's Word?

4. What does Paul mean when he says he wants to "know Christ"?

5. What exactly is prayer?

6. When should we pray?

7. Why is memorizing Scripture important? How could we begin?

CHAPTER 3
RECOGNIZING THE ENEMY'S STRATEGIES

1. According to Scripture, what are three battlefronts Christians face?

2. How can Christians expect to be treated by the world?

3. Describe the inward struggle the Christian deals with after accepting Jesus Christ as Lord and Savior.

4. What are some characteristics of a life dominated by the flesh?

5. What are some characteristics of a life obedient to the Holy Spirit?

6. What is the best way to extinguish the fiery darts of the devil?

7. Tell how the following Scriptures encourage you:
Psalm 56:9
Psalm 94:19
1 Thessalonians 3:3
1 John 4:4

CHAPTER 4
THE WAR BEGINS

1. Name the Christian's #1 enemy.

2. Name two ways truth is manifested to the believer.

3. Read Ephesians 6:10–17. What is the purpose of the breastplate?

4. Why does a Christian need feet shod with the gospel of peace?

5. Describe the helmet of salvation.

6. What is the shield of faith?

7. What is the Christian's offensive weapon? What do these Scriptures say?

Psalm 119:9
Psalm 119:11
Psalm 119:16
Psalm 119:24
Psalm 119:50
Jeremiah 23:29
Colossians 3:16

CHAPTER 5
GOING HOME

1. Why do people stray from their close relationship with God?

2. Describe how you feel when you are "out of fellowship" with someone.

3. What happened to the prodigal son when he left home?

4. Describe the father's response when he returned. What does this imply about God's love for us?

Why are the following verses meaningful to you?
Psalm 32:5
Psalm 56:9
Isaiah 43:1
Jeremiah 29:11
Jeremiah 31:3

5. What painful partings have you experienced? What did you do?

6. What does "going home" mean to a Christian?

7. When does "everlasting life" begin?
John 3:36
John 5:24

CHAPTER 6
EXAMINING THE ARENA

1. What does Paul mean when he says, "Do not be conformed to the world, but be transformed by the renewing of your minds?" (Rom. 12:1–2).

2. Write out the dictionary definition of:
conform
transform
renew

3. How can believers renew their minds?

4. What does Scripture teach regarding the world?
John 3:16
John 15:18–19
John 16:7–8
John 16:33
John 18:36
John 20:21
James 4:4

5. What symptoms of moral decay have you noticed in your lifetime?

6. How can we be "in the world" but not "of the world"?

7. Can you give a modern-day example of someone who takes a stand against evil?

CHAPTER 7
TRAINING FOR SUCCESS

1. What does it mean to be a disciple?

2. What is discipline?

3. Read Luke 14:26–27. What do these Scriptures indicate about discipleship?

4. Read 1 Timothy 4:7. Name some benefits of godly discipline.

5. What identifies us as disciples? See John 13:35, Hebrews 12:6, Galatians 5:22–25.

6. Does setting goals conflict with the will of God? Why or why not?

7. Identify goals for your life. Write out your plan for implementing them.

CHAPTER 8
GOING FOR THE GOLD

1. When does a Christian's race begin? When does it end?

2. What is endurance? What do you learn from these Scriptures?

Psalm 135:13
Psalm 136:1
Matthew 10:22
Matthew 24:13
2 Thessalonians 1:4
2 Timothy 2:10
2 Timothy 4:5
Hebrews 12:7

3. What factors in Hebrews 12:1–2 remind us to have confidence and to persevere?

4. What does it mean to "lay aside every encumbrance"?

5. According to Scripture, how should we deal with sin?

6. How can God use us as His vessels?

7. What do you think is the Christian's "gold medal"?

CHAPTER 9
BECOMING ACCOUNTABLE

1. Who is the head of the Church?

2. Name some qualities of an authentic church.

3. Compare the three main elements of the Passover with our Christian life today.

4. Why is it important to be baptized?

5. Describe the believer's proper attitude prior to taking Communion. What is the significance of the bread and the grape juice in the Lord's Supper?

6. The following Scriptures denote our responsibilities to our brothers and sisters in the body of Christ. Look up the verses and write a brief explanation in your own words.

Matthew 18:15–17
Acts 2:42
Acts 2:46
Romans 12:13
1 Corinthians 12:26
2 Corinthians 7:3
Galatians 6:2
Ephesians 4:32
Philippians 2:2
Colossians 3:16
Hebrews 10:24–25

7. Name some advantages of being part of an accountability group.

CHAPTER 10
RUNNING VICTORY LAPS

1. Read 1 Corinthians 3:10–15 and describe two kinds of believers.

2. What are some characteristics of a judge?

3. How do the attributes of God as judge differ from those of earthly judges? (Deut. 32:4, Zeph. 3:5, Ps. 89:14)

4. The words righteous and judgment often appear together in Scripture. Read Psalm 19:7–14 and identify descriptive words of:

  a. the law
  b. the results of following the law
  c. how to experience the results in your life

5. As a believer in Jesus Christ, how do these Scriptures affect your future?

  John 5:26–27
  Romans 3:26
  Romans 5:1
  Romans 5:9
  Romans 8:1
  1 Thessalonians 1:10

6. What do the following verses say regarding rewards?

  Matthew 16:27
  Luke 6:22–23
  Revelation 22:12

7. What is the *BEMA*? How will knowledge of the judgment seat of Christ affect your daily living?

CHAPTER 11
PULLING WEEDS

1. Write out Hebrews 12:15. Identify major words and phrases and explain their meaning.

2. Give one scriptural example of bitterness; and one of forgiveness. What were the long-term results?

3. Scripture gives us direction in how to respond to offenses. Read the following verses and write them in your own words:

Matthew 6:14–15
Luke 6:37
Romans 12:18
Ephesians 4:26

4. How does an unforgiving spirit affect a person's relationship with God and with others?

5. Is forgiveness a choice? Give four principles which will help us to forgive even when we don't feel like it.

6. Give some of the results which occur when people fail to forgive.

7. What offense in your life is most difficult to forgive? What response will you choose?

CHAPTER 12
BUILDING FENCES

1. Name some roaming beasts of temptations we all face.

2. Write 1 Corinthians 10:13. Identify the major phrases and tell what this verse means to you personally.

3. Read Mark 4:19. Identify three things which hinder us from a fruitful life.

4. Look up the word *holiness* or *holy*. What does it mean? How does understanding the meaning of holiness relate to the information in this chapter? Read the following verses and write the main thought:

   1 Chronicles 16:10
   John 3:30
   Romans 12:1
   1 Corinthians 3:17
   2 Corinthians 7:1
   1 Thessalonians 3:13

5. What danger faces the Christian who sits on the fence?

6. Give some reasons God sets boundaries for His children.

7. What steps can we take to stay in God's pasture?

CHAPTER 13
STAYING STEADY IN THE STORM

1. Why is suffering inevitable?

2. What was Paul's attitude toward hardships?

3. Find and write the dictionary definition of sovereignty.

4. Read these verses and write what they mean to you:
   1 Chronicles 29:11–12
   Job 42:2
   Psalm 145:13
   Ecclesiastes 7:13–14
   Isaiah 43:1–3
   Matthew 10:29–31
   Acts 17:24–26

5. How did Joseph respond to the storms in his life? (Gen. 45:5–7)

6. What are some benefits of a storm?

7. What storms are you facing in your life today? How will you choose to respond?

CHAPTER 14
ABIDING IN THE VINE

1. What are the Old Testament and the New Testament meanings attached to the vine?

2. Read John 15:1–11. Identify the following:
The vinedresser?
The vine?
The branch?

3. Give the requirements for fruit bearing.

4. What is the purpose of pruning a plant? What is the spiritual correlation?

5. *To abide in* has also been described as being *at home with*. Read the following verses and tell why you can feel comfortable with Him:
Psalm 106:1
Jeremiah 31:3
John 17:22–23
Romans 8:38–39
2 Timothy 1:9

6. Name two functions of the Holy Spirit according to John 14:26. How does this relate to "abiding"?

7. Explain how you can abide when suffering.

CHAPTER 15
HARVESTING FOR HIM

1. Explain how the agricultural concept of sowing and reaping apply to the Christian life.

2. Name some actions or reactions that hinder us from evangelism.

3. How can we become more compassionate toward others?

4. Read the following verses and write their relationship to witnessing:

Acts 1:8
Romans 10:17
1 Timothy 1:12
2 Timothy 1:7

5. What are some different methods of sowing?

6. Memorize the following verses to become better equipped:

John 1:12
John 10:9
Romans 3:23
Romans 6:23
Romans 5:8
Ephesians 2:8–9

7. If someone asked you to share your personal testimony, what would you say? Take a few minutes to outline the major points and be prepared to share it with someone.

CHAPTER 16
CELEBRATING WITH JOY!

1. What is the Christian's source of joy?

2. Read and apply these verses to the subject of joy:
   Nehemiah 8:10
   Psalm 16:11
   Luke 15:10
   John 15:11
   John 16:24
   Romans 15:13
   3 John 4
   Jude 24

3. Scripture tells us not to worry (Phil. 4:6–7). Why?

4. How is it possible to triumph in all situations (John 16:22)?

5. Read 1 Timothy 6:6 and discuss what it means to you.

6. What part of this book has meant the most to you?

7. If you could write your epitaph, what would it say?

NOTES

Chapter 1

1) J. Vernon McGee, lectures on *Romans,* delivered at Dallas Theological Seminary, Dallas, Texas, 1955.

2) Elvina M. Hall, "Jesus Paid It All," *Christian Praise Hymnal* (Nashville, Tenn.: Broadman Press, 1964).

3) William R. Newell, "At Calvary," *Christian Praise Hymnal* (Nashville, Tenn.: Broadman Press, 1964).

4) Fanny J. Crosby, "Blessed Assurance," *Christian Praise Hymnal* (Nashville, Tenn.: Broadman Press, 1964).

5) William R. Bright, ed., "Faith, Fact, Feeling," *Teacher's Manual for the Ten Basic Steps Toward Christian Maturity* (San Bernardino, Calif.: Campus Crusade for Christ, International, 1965), 215.

Chapter 2

1) Infosearch 3.0 (Abraham Lincoln story).

Chapter 3

1) Cabell Phillips, *The 1940s: Decade of Triumph and Trouble* (New York: Macmillian, 1975), 64–65.

2) Charles H. Colson with Nancy A. Pearcey, *A Dangerous Grace: Daily Readings* (Dallas, Tex.: Word Publishing, 1994), 327.

3) Ibid.

4) Dr. Jim Black, *When Nations Die* (Wheaton, Ill.: Tyndale House, 1994), 14–15.

5) Neil Anderson, *The Bondage Breaker* (Eugene, Ore.: Harvest House, 1990), 82–83.

6) Ibid.

Chapter 4

1) Cornelius Ryan, *The Longest Day* (New York: Fawcett Popular Library Books, 1959), 103–05.

2) Brooke Foss Westcott, *St. Paul's Epistle to the Ephesians* (Grand Rapids, Mich.: Wm. B. Eerdmans, 1960), 64.

3) Warren Wiersbe, *Prayer, Praise, and Promises—A Daily Walk through the Psalms* (Grand Rapids, Mich.: Baker Book House, 1992), 199.

4) Charles H. Colson, *Life Sentence* (Lincoln, Va.: Chosen Books, 1979), 21.

CHAPTER 5

1) Billy Graham, *Facing Death and the Life After* (Minneapolis, Minn.: Grayson, 1987), 224.

2) J. R. Miller, *Words of Comfort* (Ridgefield, N.J.: AMG Publishers, n.d.), 12.

3) Charles H. Spurgeon, *Faith's Checkbook* (Chicago, Ill.: Moody Press, 1987), 95.

CHAPTER 6

1) Black, *When Nations Die.*

2) Bob Paulson, "The Legacy of Eric Liddell: 'Strive for the Best,'" *Decision,* February 1995, 27.

3) Abraham Lincoln, quoted in *Webster's World Dictionary of Quotable Definitions,* (n.p., n.d.).

4) David T. Moore, lecture delivered at Palm Desert Community Church, Palm Desert, California, July 2, 1993.

5) William J. Bennett, *The Index of Leading Cultural Indicators* (New York: Simon and Schuster, 1994), 73–74.

6) Moore, lecture.

7) Bennett, *The Index of Leading Cultural Indicators.*

8) Dave Dravecky with Tim Stafford, "Who Am I Pitching For?" *Moody Magazine,* September 1990, 20–23.

9) Michelle Hopkins, "Wally Frost, An Active Dad in a Wheelchair," *Family Life Today,* July–August 1981, 8–11.

10) Moore, lecture.

11) Paul Tan, *Encyclopedia of 7700 Illustrations: Signs of the Times* (Rockville, Md.: Assurance Publishers, 1984), 1458.

12) Abraham Lincoln, letter reprinted in *One Hundred and One Famous Poems,* comp. Roy J. Cook (Chicago, Ill.: Contemporary Books, Inc., 1958), 177.

CHAPTER 7

1) Walter A. Henrichson, *Disciples Are Made, Not Born* (Wheaton, Ill.: Victor Books, 1974), 18.

2) Harry Verploegh, ed., *The Oswald Chambers Devotional Reader* (Nashville, Tenn.: Thomas Nelson Publishers, 1990), 71.

3) Ibid., 75.

4) Dennis Waitley, *Timing Is Everything* (Nashville, Tenn.: Thomas Nelson Publishers, 1992), 12.

CHAPTER 8

1) Source unknown.

2) Charles E. Jones, *Life Is Tremendous!* (Wheaton, Ill.: Tyndale House, 1970), 54.

3) Dravecky with Stafford, "Who Am I Pitching For?"

4) Ibid.

5) F. B. Meyer, *The Way into the Holiest* (Westchester, Ill.: Good News, 1960), 43.

6) Steven Lawson, *Men Who Win: Pursuing the Ultimate Prize* (Colorado Springs, Colo.: NavPress, 1992), 15.

CHAPTER 9

1) Infosearch 3.1.

2) Charles H. Colson with Ellen Santilli Vaughn, *The Body* (Dallas, Tex.: Word Publishing, 1992), 129.

3) Paula D'Arcy, *Where the Wind Begins* (Wheaton, Ill.: Harold Shaw Publishers, 1984), 46.

4) John Mohr, "Find Us Faithful" (Birdwing Music/Jonathan Mark Music, 1987, administered by the Sparrow Corporation), quoted in Calvin Miller, *Walking with Saints: Through the Best and Worst Times of Our Lives* (Nashville, Tenn.: Thomas Nelson Publishers, 1995), 192.

CHAPTER 10

1) "The Thrill of Victory," *Greenville* (Texas) Herald Banner, May 26, 1996.

2) J. I. Packer, *Knowing God* (Downers Grove, Ill.: InterVarsity Press, 1973), 127–28.

3) Dr. Joe L. Wall, *Going for the Gold* (Chicago, Ill.: Moody Press, 1991), 11–12.

4) Horatio G. Spafford, "It Is Well with My Soul," *Christian Praise Hymnal* (Nashville, Tenn.: Broadman Press, 1964).

5) Fran Caffey Sandin, *See You Later, Jeffrey* (Wheaton, Ill.: Tyndale House, 1988), 102.

6) Wall, *Gold,* 33.

7) Ibid., 21–22.

8) Source unknown.

9) Tyler (Texas) *Morning Telegraph,* April 16, 1996.

CHAPTER 11

1) James R. Upp Sr., M.D., "The Ultimate Test of Forgiveness," *The Christian Medical and Dental Society Journal,* March–April 1994, 28–30.

2) "Never Give Up," *Insight for Living,* Winter 1986, 27.

3) David V. Kiel as told to Ann Lunde, "I'm Learning How to Forgive," *Decision,* February 1986, 12–13.

4) David Augsburger, *The Freedom of Forgiveness, 70 x 7* (Chicago: Moody Press), 26.

5) Lewis B. Smedes, *Forgive and Forget: Healing the Hurts We Don't Deserve* (New York: Pocket Books, 1984), xii.

6) Dan B. Allender and Tremper Longman, III, *Bold Love* (Colorado Springs, Colo.: NavPress, 1992), 42.

7) Frances A. Schaeffer, *The Mark of the Christian* (Downers Grove, Ill.: InterVarsity Press, 1970), 24.

8) Paul Adolph, *Release from Tension* (Chicago: Moody Bible Institute of Chicago, 1956), 87.

9) Smedes, *Forgive and Forget,* 131.

10) Upp, "The Ultimate Test of Forgiveness."

11) "Never Give Up," *Insight for Living.*

12) Kiel, "I'm Learning How to Forgive."

CHAPTER 12

1) Sheldon Vanauken, *A Severe Mercy* (New York: Harper Collins, 1977), 53–54.

2) Rod Sargent, *Christians in the Making* (Colorado Springs, Colo.: NavPress, 1981), 10.

3) Elisabeth Elliot, *Shadow of the Almighty: The Life and Testament of Jim Elliot* (New York: Harper and Row, 1958), 15, 247.

4) Karl Menninger quoted in Charles Swindoll, *Active Spirituality* (Dallas, Tex.: Word Publishing, 1994), 144.

5) Hannah Hurnard, *Mountain of Spices* (Wheaton, Ill.: Tyndale House, 1977), 91.

CHAPTER 13

1) Pearl Anderson, "Suffering," used by permission.

2) Spiros Zodhiates, *The Behavior of Belief: An Exposition of James Based upon the Original Greek Text* (Grand Rapids, Mich.: Wm. B. Eerdmans, 1959), 33.

3) Max Lucado, *In the Eye of the Storm* (Dallas, Tex.: Word Publishing, 1991), 187.

4) R. Kelso Carter, "Standing on the Promises," *Christian Praise Hymnal* (Nashville, Tenn.: Broadman Press, 1964).

CHAPTER 14

1) C. S. Lovett, *Lights for Laymen,* (n.p., n.d.).

2) William R. Bright, *Revolution Now* (San Bernardino, Calif.: Campus Crusade for Christ, 1969), 68–69.

3) David Brainerd, *The Life and Diary of David Brainerd* quoted in ed. E. Glenn Hinson, *Doubleday Devotional Classics, Volume II,* (Garden City, N.Y.: Doubleday, 1978), 477.

4) Stephen Olford, *I'll Take the High Road* (Grand Rapids, Mich.: Zondervan, 1968, renewed in 1996 by Stephen F. Olford), n.p.

5) Mary E. Maxwell, "Channels Only," *The New Church Hymnal* (Newbury Park, Calif.: Lexicon Music, 1976).

6) W. Phillip Keller, *A Gardener Looks at the Fruits of the Spirit* (Waco, Tex.; Word Books, 1979), 44–45.

7) Annie Johnson Flint, quoted in V. Raymond Edman, in *The Disciplines of Life* (USA: Scripture Press, 1948), 228.

8) Jim Elliot quoted in Elisabeth Elliot, *Shadow of the Almighty: The Life and Testament of Jim Elliot* (New York: Harper and Row, 1958), 247.

9) E. Margaret Clarkson, "So Send I You," *The New Church Hymnal* (Newbury Park, Calif.: Lexicon Music, 1976).

CHAPTER 15

1) John Baird quoted in *Reaching Men Ministries Newsletter,* February 1995.

2) John G. Mitchell, *An Everlasting Love* (Portland, Ore.: Multnomah Press, 1982), 83.

3) Bill Hull, *Building High Commitment in a Low-Commitment World* (Grand Rapids, Mich.: Fleming H. Revell, 1995), 67.

4) D. L. Moody, source unknown.

5) Steven J. Lawson, *Men Who Win* (Colorado Springs, Colo.: NavPress, 1992), 151.

6) Charles H. Spurgeon, *The Treasury of the Bible* (Grand Rapids, Mich.: Zondervan, 1962), 800.

7) Mohr, "Find Us Faithful."

CHAPTER 16

1) Larry Beal, used by permission.

2) John MacKinnon, used by permission.

3) Walt Huntley, "God's Hall of Fame" quoted in Bobby Richardson, *The Bobby Richardson Story* (Westwood, N.J.: Fleming H. Revell, 1965), 155–56.

4) Mark Twain, quoted in Albert M. Wells Jr., *Inspiring Quotations* (Nashville, Tenn.: Thomas Nelson Publishers, 1988), 220.

5) Bill Gothard, Basic Youth Conflicts Seminar.

6) Haddon Robinson, quoted in Albert M. Wells, Jr., *Inspiring Quotations.*

7) Corrie ten Boom, quoted in Albert M. Wells, Jr., *Inspiring Quotations.*

8) François Fenelon, *Let Go* (Springdale, Pa.: Whitaker House, 1973), 10–11.

9) George Bernard Shaw, quoted in Stephen R. Covey, *Principle-Centered Leadership* (New York: Simon and Schuster, 1990), 324.